YOU CAN DRAW MANGA

with
BEN DUNN, DAVID HUTCHISON & ROD ESPINOSA

© 2005 Antarctic Press

Published by Mud Puddle Books, Inc.
54 West 21st Street
Suite 601
New York, New York 10010
info@mudpuddlebooks.com

ISBN: 1-59412-104-4

Printed in the United States of America

KONNICHIWA! HA! BET YOU DIDN'T THINK I KNEW ANY JAPAN
DID YOU! ALL KIDDING ASIDE... I DON'T! WHAT I DO KNOW
THAT I LOVE THE "MANGA" STYLE OF DRAWING! I SAY "MAN
BECAUSE THERE ARE CERTAIN CHARACTERISTICS THAT SEPA
IT FROM TRADITIONAL WESTERN COMICS. MORE ON THAT IN
LATER CHAPTERS. WHAT I'LL COVER HERE ARE THE ELEMENT
MANGA THAT I HAVE CHOSEN TO USE IN MY OWN ART STYL
I DO NOT PROFESS THIS TO BE THE ONLY WAY TO DO IT. B
YOU WILL SEE THAT IT USES BASIC ELEMENTS THAT APPLY
TO ALL STYLES. SO LET'S NOT WASTE ANY MORE TIME! LET
ART MANGA!

TOOLS OF THE TRADE!

BEFORE ONE CAN DRAW, ONE MUST HAVE
THE RIGHT TOOLS. USE WHAT IS AVAILABLE!
ADAPT WITH WHAT YOU KNOW. FOR ME, THE
MOST COMMON TOOLS I DRAW WITH ARE:
STAEDTLER PIGMENT LINERS (SIZES 01, 03, 05
AND 07), A ZEBRA 0.5 MECHANICAL PENCIL,
TYPE HB LEAD, PARALLEL GLIDER RULER,
LARGE RAISED-EDGE TRIANGLE, MARS MAGIC
RUB ERASER, PEN BRUSH, OPAQUE BLACK INDIA
INK, WHITE OUT, WHITE INK, OLD TOOTH-
BRUSHES, RAISED-EDGE FRENCH CURVE, VARIOUS
CIRCLE AND OVAL TEMPLATES, RAISED-EDGE
RULER, FINE-POINT SHARPIE MARKERS, OLD
RAGS, TWO LARGE JARS FILLED WITH WATER
(ONE FOR CLEANING BLACK INK AND ONE FOR
CLEANING WHITE INK), 15-INCH T-SQUARE AND
2-PLY, SMOOTH-SURFACE BRISTOL BOARD.
GOT IT? GOOD, LET'S CONTINUE ON.

THE ENVIRONMENT

SURROUNDINGS ARE VERY IMPORTANT TO ME.
I PREFER AN AREA RELATIVELY CLEAN, A
SMOOTH DRAWING SURFACE WITH GOOD LIGHT,
AND A TAPE DECK TO POUND OUT SOME TUNES
DURING THOSE LATE-NIGHT DRAWING SHIFTS.
THIS IS WHAT WORKS FOR ME WHEN I AM IN
SERIOUS DRAWING MODE. YOU WILL FIND THAT
THE FEWER DISTRACTIONS YOU HAVE, THE MORE
YOU CAN CONCENTRATE
ON YOUR DRAWING!
HOWEVER, USE WHAT
YOU CAN AND ADAPT!
FOR YEARS I DREW ON
THE KITCHEN TABLE
OR ON THE FLOOR!

ATTITUDE!
THIS IS THE MOST IMPORTANT INGREDIENT!
IF YOU HAVE NO DESIRE TO DRAW OR IMPROVE,
THEN STOP RIGHT HERE! OTHERWISE, YOU MUST
NOT GIVE UP! PERFECTION ONLY COMES WITH
PRACTICE, PRACTICE, PRACTICE! EVEN I AM
STILL LEARNING NEW TRICKS!
YOUR LEVEL OF SKILL IS GOING TO BE, I ASSUME,
STILL AT THE BEGINNER'S STAGE. THINGS
LIKE PERSPECTIVE AND ANATOMY WILL COME
LATER IN THIS SERIES. IF YOU KNOW SOME OF
IT ALREADY, GREAT! IF NOT, DON'T WORRY,
WE WILL COVER THAT SOON ENOUGH!

OU CAN DRAW MANGA

Drawing The Face

It is important to have a good idea where everything on the face rests in relation to the other features from both the front and the side. You may think that, since you are going to be drawing huge eyes and tiny mouths and noses, this is not important. On the contrary, it is even mc critical to be aware of the proper location of the major facial features before you start to change them around. This will ensure that your fac proprtions maintain visual consistency.

Front View

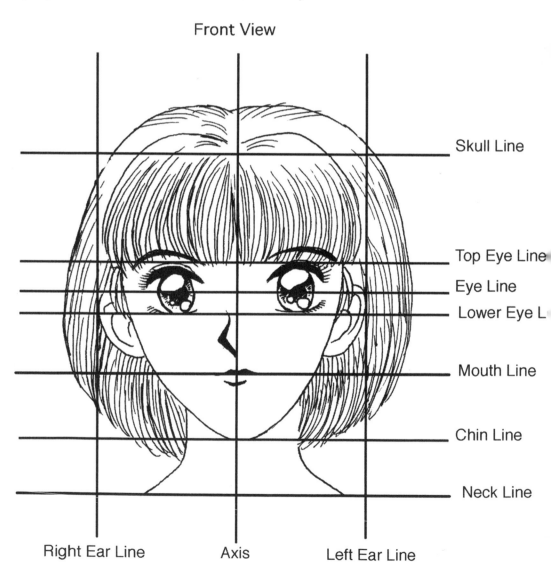

Skull Line

Top Eye Line

Eye Line

Lower Eye L

Mouth Line

Chin Line

Neck Line

Right Ear Line   Axis   Left Ear Line

Drawing The Face

here are a lot of lines going across this head, as there were on the last one. hese lines are to help you understand where objects on a face rest in relation each other. For instance, the center of the eye is approximately aligned ith the center of the ear. By understanding these proportions, we an see that even if you are drawing huge eyes and tiny ears, if the center each lines up, you are creating a face that will be following the uidelines of a normal face.

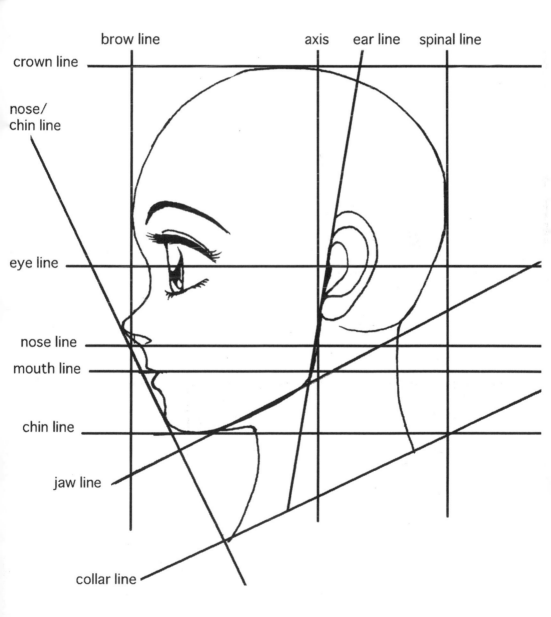

Gender Differences In Heads

There are obvious differences in facial structure and proportions between male and female faces and heads. In shoujo, you are free to reduce those differences as much as you want in the pursuit of creating bishounen, but it is best to understand what the differences in facial structure are before you start experimenting.

Female eyes are bigger with more lashes.
They have a softer curve to their face, and
petite noses, their mouths are smaller,
and they have thin necks. They generally
have more highlights in their hair.

Gender Differences In Heads

Males tend to have smaller eyes, sharper facial features, longer faces, slightly larger noses, bigger mouths, and thicker necks.

Remember, in shoujo, you are free to blend the features of men and women as much as you like.

Mouths

Refering back to the proportions drawing, we see that the mouth usually lies halfway between the tip of the chin and the bottom of the eyes. In shoujo, the mouth is often understated and almost invisible when closed. This can change quickly when the character becomes excited, and the mouth can become ridiculously large.

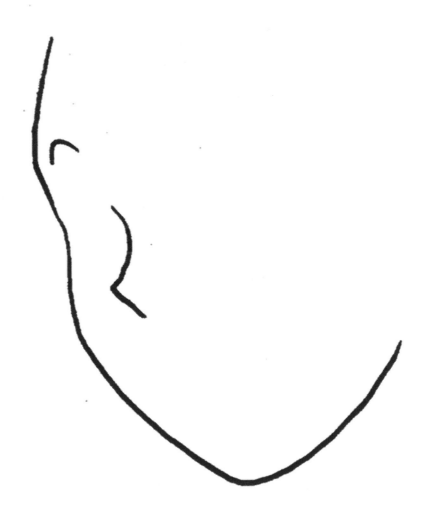

Here we have a basic face template to which we can add mouths. When you start expressing strong emotion, you enter a whole different arena, and face shape is pretty much up to you.

YOU CAN DRAW MANGA

Mouths

We have placed two closed mouths, one with and one without lipstick.

Mouths

On this face, we have an open
mouth yelling. Notice that it is
not necessary to separate
the individual teeth. Also,
notice how the mouth opens
down and the top of the mouth
stays in the same position.

Eyes

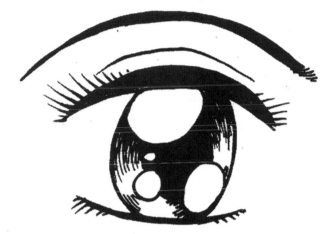

Here are two example eyes for quick reference. First, notice that the eyebrow extends around the pupil. Then, notice the light reflecting off of the iris. This is especially common in shoujo, and the more light that is reflected, the more intense the emotions of the current scene are.

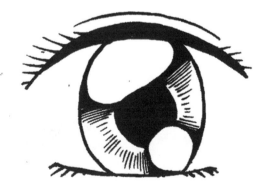

Note how these two eyes each use different styles of iris. The top is a scratch method iris, with lines being drawn around the pupil. The bottom is a radial iris, with lines being drawn out from the pupil.

By playing with the shape of the eye, you can create a wide range of emotions and effects.

Eyes

When you draw the eye, a smart way to begin i
with a simple circle. Using that circle to build o
you can construct the entire eye, from highlight
to eyelashes. An important thing to remember
when you draw eyes is that the circle you start
with will change in shape as the character's
head turns and moves, like the example below

Eyes

First, you want to begin with the outside shape of the eye, then work your way inward, drawing the line for the pupil.

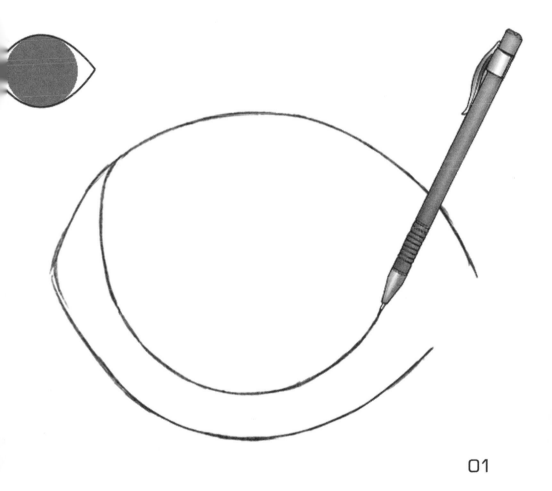

01

Eyes

Next, the circle for the iris should be drawn in the center of the pupil.

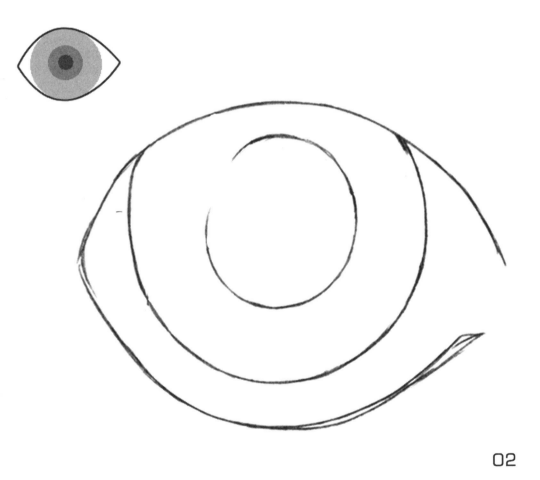

02

Eyes

Now it's time to lay out the high-lights. So what are highlights? Highlights are where the light is reflected off of a surface. A great trick to highlights is to draw a set of them that look good and use them every time you draw eyes, a reflective ball (if you can find one) can help you figure out highlights.

03

Eyes

Now that the eye and highlights are drawn, it's time for the extras. The eyebrow should typically follow the contour of the top line of the eye. When it comes to eyelashes, you should approach them as a single mass. The top eyelid lashes will be a larger mass than the lower eyelid lashes. Finally, draw in the shadows using the top lid to guide you.

04

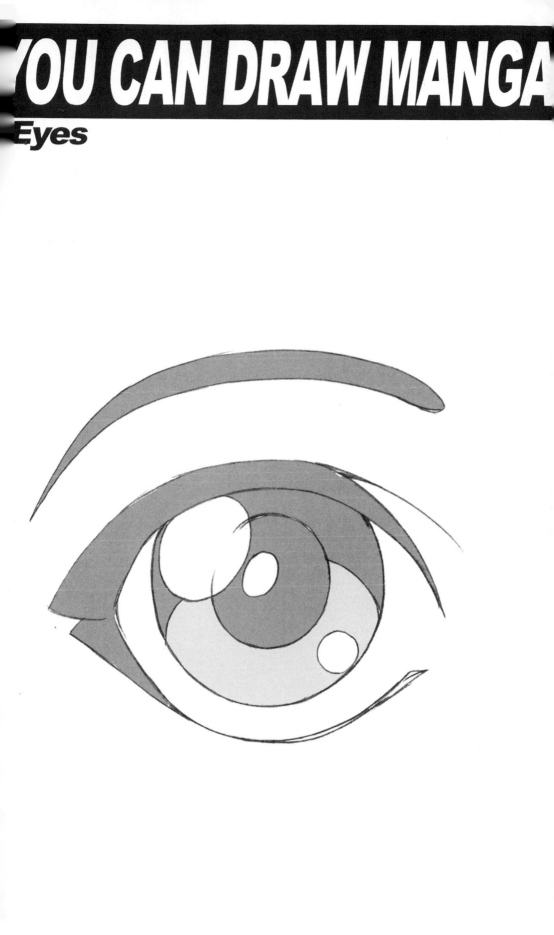

19

Eyes

There are many ways to draw eyes, and the way you draw the eyes in manga is a strong indicator of the personality of your characters. Typically, rounded shapes tend to belong to the characters that are the heroes or heroines. Angles are used for the characters that are evil or whose motives are questionable or unknown.

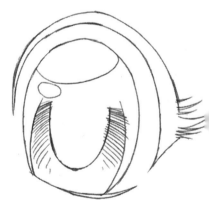

YOU CAN DRAW MANGA

Eyes

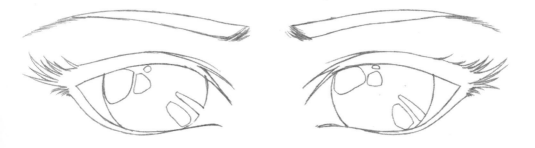

Eyes

When you're drawing your many characters, there will be times wh
you have to draw older characters. A good rule of thumb is the mo
lines you draw around a person's eyes, the older they will look. Wh
you're drawing the wrinkles around the eyes, the lines should follov
the contours of the outside of the eye. As you can see, the lines orig
nate in the same places in the corners of the eyes and progressivel
droop downward.

23

Eyes

Eyes

When placing eyes on a face, be sure that the line of the eyebrow extends through to the line of the nose, even if you erase most of the nose. As your drawing nears completion, this guideline is a good idea when first placing the major facial features.

You can either place the eyes or the nose first, but remember either way you do it, their lines need to be in agreement.

Eyes

Here's a couple of different examples of how the center guideline can be used to draw the eyes.

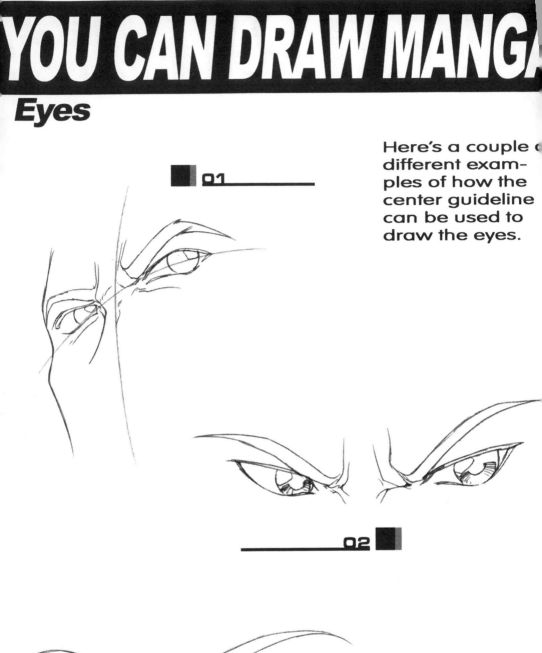

01

02

03

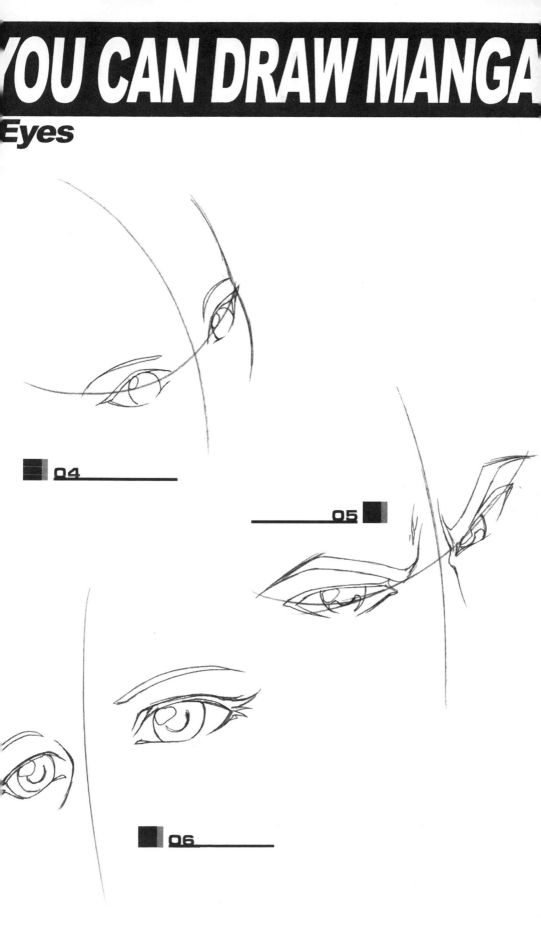

04

05

06

YOU CAN DRAW MANGA

Breaking Down The Nose

Drawing the manga nose is an exercise in minimalism. Starting with a traditionally rendered nose, you can begin to break it down into basic seperations. By stripping away all the other lines, leaving only the line for the bridge of the nose and the shadow underneath, we start to develop the beginnings of a manga nose. From this point, you can minimize the nose even more, depending on your tastes.

01

YOU CAN DRAW MANGA
Breaking Down The Nose

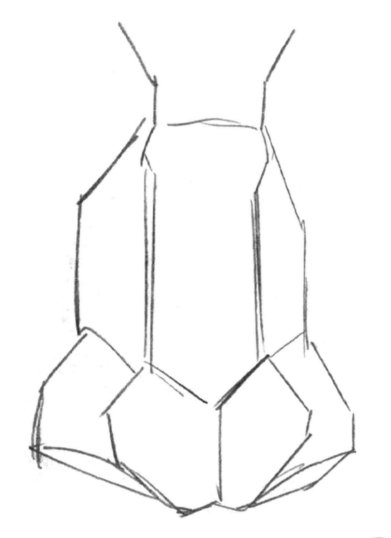

02

Breaking Down The Nose

03

Breaking Down The Nose

04

Breaking Down The Nose

05

The Mouth

Drawing the guideline for the mouth is determined by splitting the difference between the bottom eye line and the bottom of the chin. That mouth line would be where the middle of the mouth is. We'll talk more about drawing the mouth later.

The Mouth

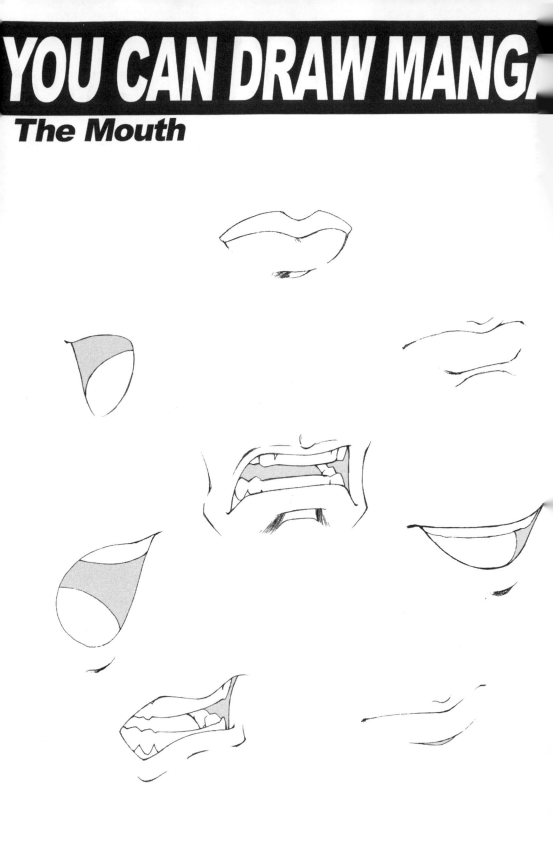

yes

Because of the simple structure of the manga style face, there are many, many ways to express emotion.

Here are a few examples of the more common emotions on very simple faces. The key characteristics to look for are the shape and placement of the mouth and the shape and placement of the eyebrows.

apologetic

Eyes

Eyebrows and eyelids tilted
upwards give off a negative
emotion on the face
of a character.

sad

shocked or

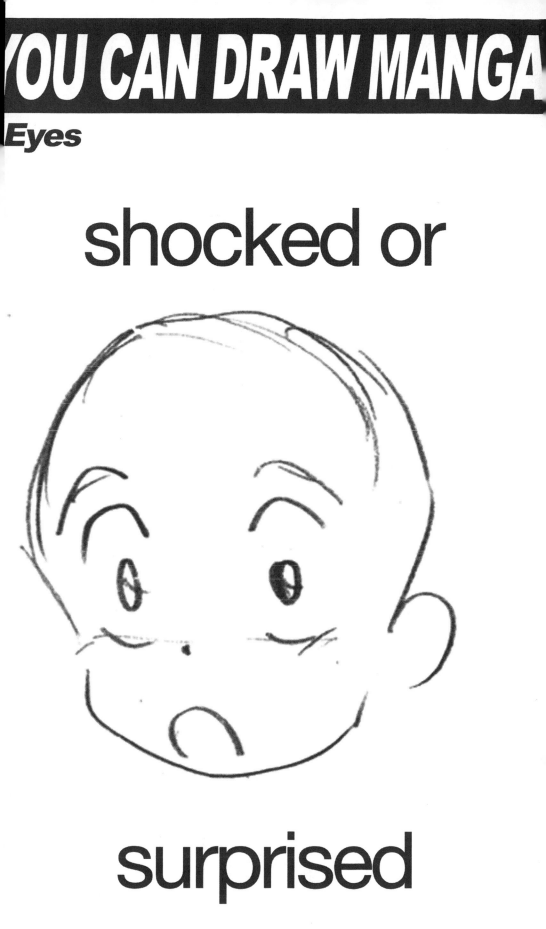

surprised

Eyes

These emotions all have downward-curving eyebrows. This is usually a sign of negative emotion like anger or sadistic glee.

crackling

angry

gritting

Eyes

These three examples
demonstrate positive emotions.

very happy or excited

Eyes

happy or

pleased

Eyes

The tilted eyebrows combined with
a smiling mouth complete the effect.

modest

Eyes

wily

Expressions

Blush

WHEN NORMAL BLUSHING SIMPLY ISN'T ENOUGH, YOU CAN MAKE A CHARACTER CUTER BY ADDING BLUSH CIRCLES. MORE OFTEN THAN NOT, THESE CIRCLES ARE SEEN ON YOUNGER CHARACTERS. SOMETIMES THEY ARE USED AS A PART OF THE CHARACTER DESIGN.

Expressions

Veins

THIS TYPE OF VEIN IS OFTEN USED TO DENOTE AN ANNOYED CHARACTER. TYPICALLY A COMICAL ELEMENT, THEY ARE USED BOTH ON AND OFF OF THE BODY. YOU DON'T JUST HAVE TO USE THESE ON THE FOREHEAD.

Expressions

Steam

THIS IS A COMMON DEVICE IN BOTH AMERICAN AND JAPANESE COMICS. STEAM HAS ANY NUMBER OF USES, SOME OF WHICH WILL BE COVERED LATER.

Swirls

THESE TYPES OF SWIRLS ARE OFTEN USED TO SHOW THAT SOMETHING IS WRONG INSIDE THE CHARACTER, EITHER MENTALLY OR PHYSICALLY.

Expressions

Sparks

GENERALLY, SPARKS ARE USED
TO SHOW RECOGNITION OR
SUDDEN AWARENESS OF A
SITUATION.

Expressions

Tears

TEARS OF THE TYPE TO
THE LEFT ARE USED FOR
MORE COMICAL SITUATIONS.
YOU DON'T USUALLY SEE
THIS TYPE IN SERIOUS
STORIES.

Expressions

NOW LET'S TAKE A LOOK AT HOW SOME OF THESE IDEAS CAN BE COMBINED. HERE ARE SOME EXAMPLES OF OVERLAPPING DEVICES USED IN VARIOUS SITUATIONS.

IN THIS INSTANCE, WE'LL GO BACK TO OUR TEAR EXAMPLE. I JUST WANTED TO POINT OUT THAT WITH A SIMPLE SWITCH OF THE EYEBROWS, WE CAN MAKE OUR CHARACTER'S PERSONALITY COMPLETELY CHANGE FROM TOTALLY BROKEN TO BOUND AND DETERMINED.

＊ BILLY LATER LOST THE TOURNAMENT.

Expressions

THE SAME IS TRUE IN THIS EXAMPLE.

Expressions

HERE ARE SOME OTHER SITUATIONS
YOU COULD PUT YOUR CHARACTERS IN:

SHOULD I TAKE
THE CAR? OR
WHAT'S BEHIND
DOOR NUMBER
TWO?

YOU CAN DRAW MANGA

Expressions

YOU CAN DRAW MANGA

Expressions

Expressions

HERE IS A MORE
TRADITIONAL USE FOR
TEARS. MANGA
CHARACTERS TEND TO
TEAR UP A LOT FROM
EMOTION AND STRESS.

I DON'T
BELIEVE
IT!

SEARCH
YOUR
FEELINGS...
YOU KNOW
IT TO BE
TRUE!

Expressions

MANGA, AS WITH ANY ENTERTAINMENT
MEDIUM, IS BUILT AROUND THE READER
IDENTIFYING WITH THE CHARACTERS.
THUS, AS SOON AS A PROTAGANIST ENTE
A BAD SITUATON, THEY BEGIN TO SWEAT
SHAKE, AND DISPLAY OTHER VARIOUS
FORMS OF INTERNAL DISCOMFORT.

Expressions

WHEN A CHARACTER COMES TO
A REALIZATON OR UNDERSTANDING,
OR WHEN THEY ARE SURPRISED OR
OTHERWISE CAUGHT OFF GUARD,
YOU WILL USUALLY SEE SOME
TYPE OF SPARK EFFECT TO
INDICATE IT VISUALLY.

Expressions

IN THESE TWO EXAMPLES, THE MOOD OF THE SITUATION CAN BE MANIPULATED BY EXCHANGING THE REACTIONS OF THE CHARACTER AND REWRITING THE DIALOGUE.

Expressions

IT'S GOOD TO DO THESE EXERCISES IN ORDER TO LEARN ABOUT THE KIND OF FLEXIBILITY THAT AN ARTIST OR WRITER CAN HAVE IN THEIR STORIES.

Expressions

I THINK BLUSH IS USED FAR TOO MUCH IN MANGA-INSPIRED ARTWOR
IT IS NOT OFTEN USED AS IT SHOULD BE, TO INDICATE A BLUSH,
BUT AS A FACIAL DETAIL. MANY TIMES, THE ARTIST WILL USE LINES
TO SHOW THE PLANE OF THE NOSE AND CHEEKS, AND IT CAN BE
DIFFICULT TO TELL THE DIFFERENCE IF YOU AREN'T CAREFUL.

Expressions

THERE ARE A COUPLE OF DETAILS IN THIS EXAMPLE THAT I WANT TO REFER TO, BUT FOR NOW I JUST WANT TO MENTION THE CHEEK LINES ON THE FACE. THESE ARE JUST SKETCHY INDICATIONS OF THE SURFACE OF THE CHEEKS.

Expressions

HERE'S SOMETHING YOU CAN DO TO SHOW YOUR CHARACTER'S FACE FROM TWO DIFFERENT POINTS OF VIEW.

IN THIS CASE, YOU CAN DRAW A NORMAL FRONT VIEW. ONCE YOU'V DRAWN THE OUTER FORM, ALL YO NEED TO DO IS ADJUST FACIAL RELATIONS.

HERE, THE CHARACTER'S FACE IS SLIGHTLY UPTURNED. SIMPLY MOVE ALL OF THE FACIAL ELEMENTS CLOSER TO THE FOREHEAD.

IN THIS SHOT, DRAW THE FACIAL ELEMENTS CLOSER TO THE BOTTOM OF THE HEAD TO MAKE THE CHARACTER'S HEAD SEEM TO BE DOWNTURNED.

YOU CAN DRAW MANGA

Applying Hair

We have talked a great deal about different hairstyles, heads, and rotation, so next we need to combine them and talk about applying hair to your character's head.

First, draw a hairline on your character's head. This will act as a guide to placing the hairstyle you have selected.

Applying Hair

Second, decide on your hairstyle.

* Your highlights should follow the curve of the hair.

Applying Hair

Third, draw the basic shape of the hairstyle.

* Feathering the edge
of the sheen gives the
illusion of strands of
hair.

Applying Hair

Fourth, start drawing hair. Be sure to use thin lines so that you don't get fat hair.

*Separating the edges of the
hair also gives the impression
of individual strands

Body Types

here are as many different body types as there are people, but in shoujo and
nanga in general, there are a number of body types that appear fairly frequently.
he two most frequent shoujo types are adolescent-like in shape.

Adolescent Female

Most shoujo characters
are adolescents or at least
depicted that way. Hips on
women are not very
pronounced and breasts
tend toward the smaller
side.

Body Types

Adolescent Male

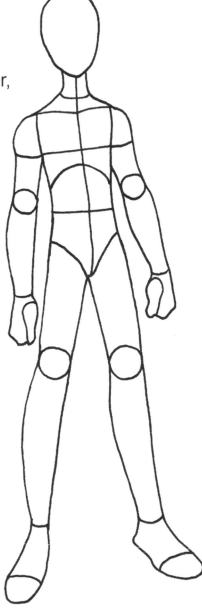

Males tend to be slender, tall, and not overly muscular, as opposed to the way they are often seen in shounen manga.

Body Types

Adult Female

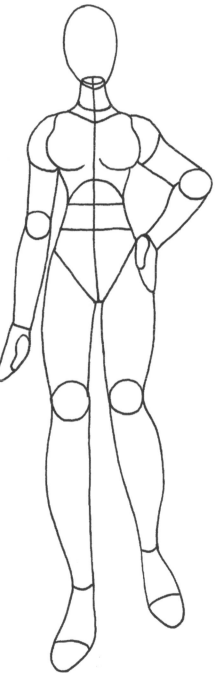

Averge body type adult male and
male characters do make frequent
appearances in shoujo manga,
usually in supporting roles.
Parents, teachers, and any
number of outside adult
influences share these
body types.

Body Types

Adult Male

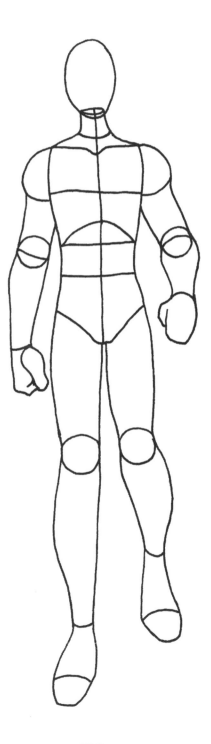

Body Types

Chances are pretty good that a muscle-bound character will pop up at some point. This body type is common among bullies, gym teachers, the heads of sports clubs, and possibly annoying older brothers.

Muscular Male

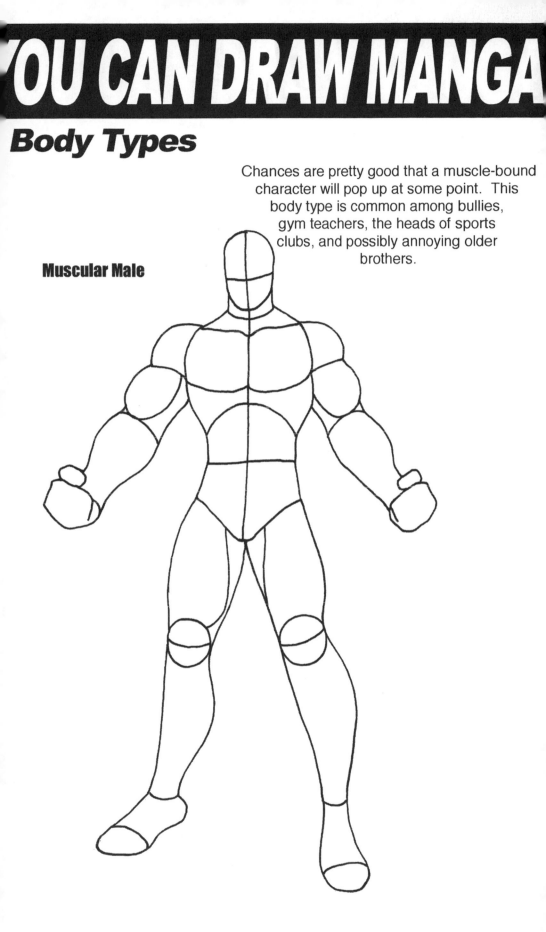

Body Types

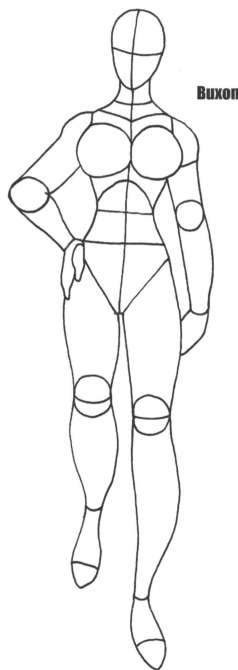

Buxom Female

The buxom female is another body type usually found in antagonists. Anyone from an older woman distracting your character's romantic interest to an evil temptress in a magical girl story can have this body type.

Body Types

Male Child

the characters in your story are really young, you will want to use the child body type.

Body Types

Female Child

The key to drawing
this body type is that
by enlarging the head,
you can make a figure
appear to be younger
in age.

Body Types

Chibi

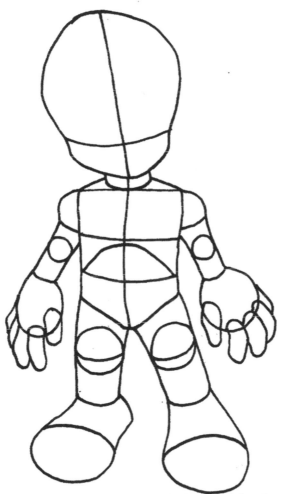

The chibi, or super deformed body type, is a visual tool common to all manga, shoujo or shounen. It is used in a variety of ways, but the figure usually has a very small body and a very large head.

Hands and Feet

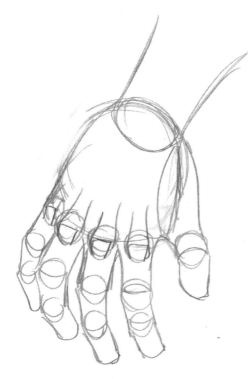

Looking at these drawings makes the hand look very complicated. The key to drawing the hand well is properly understanding the anatomy.

But if you don't want to study anatomy (which you really ought to), here's an easy way to approach drawing them.

Hands and Feet

egin by drawing a circle for the palm of the hand. Look at your own
and for the placement of the lines that will later become the fingers.
en draw an oval to represent the thick part of the palm where the
umb connects. Use small circles to place the knuckles and cylinders
r the fingers. After you've constructed the hand, you can then start
ndering, use your own hand for a model.

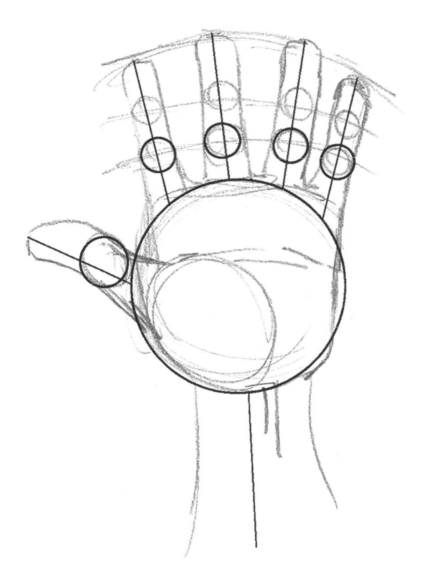

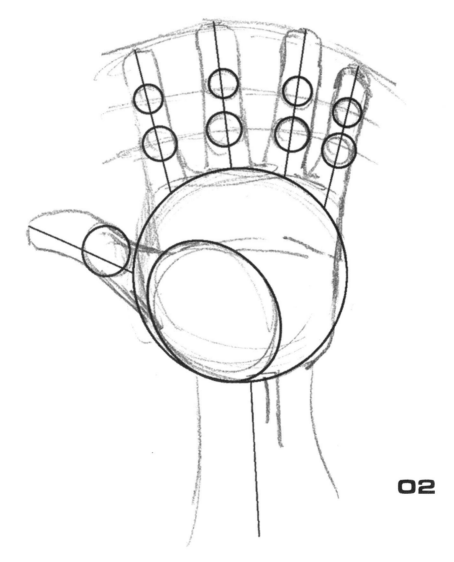

02

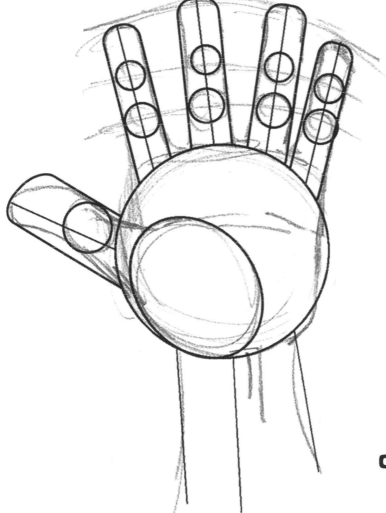

03

Hands and Feet

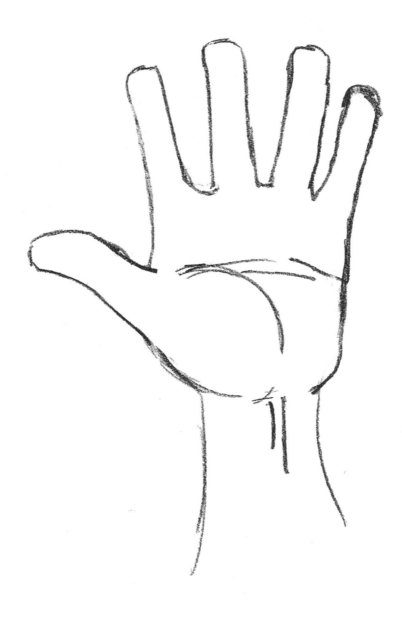

Hands and Feet

When you're drawing the hand in different poses, the same princi-ples apply. The difference is the use and understanding of cylinders becomes more important. As you can see below, the cylinders used for the fingers and forearm are drawn in perspective. Drawing the fingers individually using this approach will help you get the pose right and add the illusion of depth.

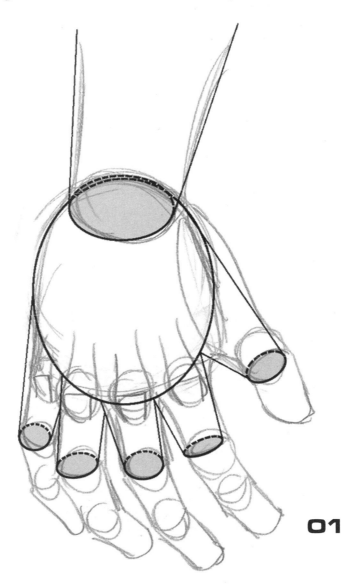

01

Hands and Feet

When you're drawing the hand in different poses, the same principles apply. The difference is the use and understanding of cylinder becomes more important. As you can see below, the cylinders used for the fingers and forearm are drawn in perspective. Drawing the fingers individually using this approach will help you get the pose right and add the illusion of depth.

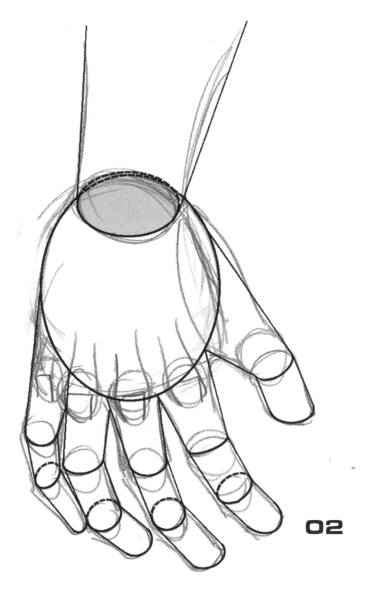

02

82

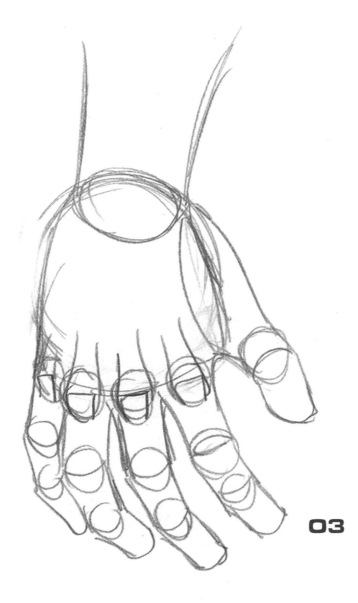

03

Hands and Feet

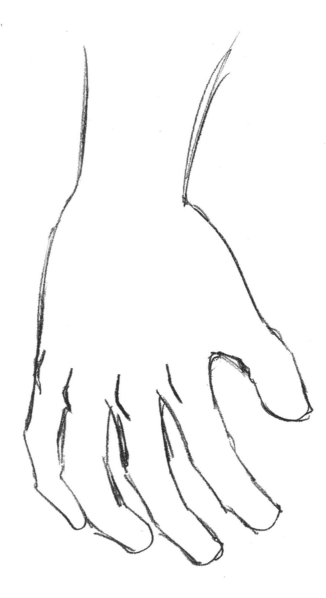

Hands and Feet

Once you are able to understand how the hand and
fingers work, you'll be able to
apply that understanding to
drawing the rest of the arm.
Pose in a mirror or have
someone pose for you, and
take pictures in the pose
you're trying to draw.

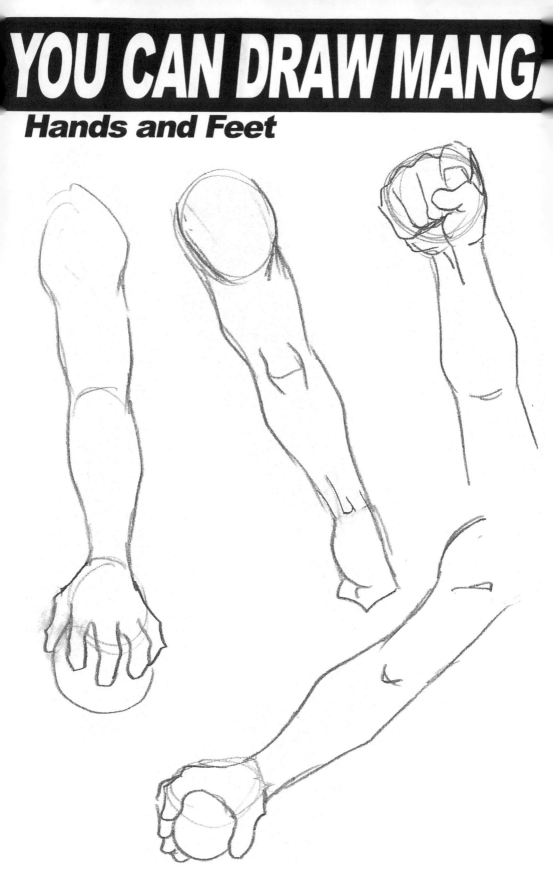

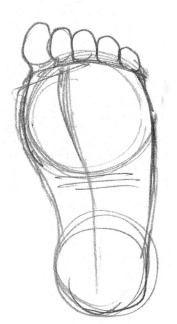

Feet may look simple, but once you get down to it, they tend to be a little more difficult than drawing hands.

From the bottom of the foot, they are much simpler than hands, but when you look at them the way they are normally seen, the complexity shows.

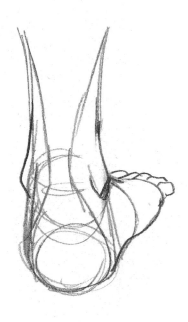

Hands and Feet

Feet generally can be broken down to two circles: a large circle for the "ball" of the foot and a circle about 1/3 smaller for the heel. Then you draw five circles for the toes, each one getting progressively smaller than the last. Then, you connect the front and back of the foot by drawing the arch and outside of the foot. Like I said before, this is probably the easiest pose the foot could be in, but it is the least common.

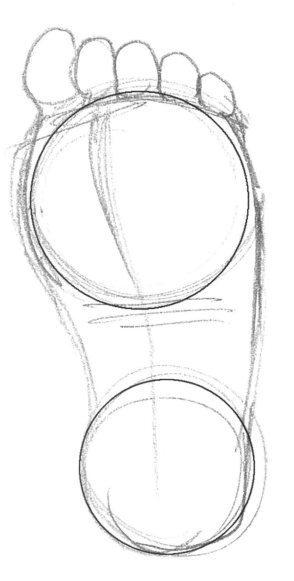

01

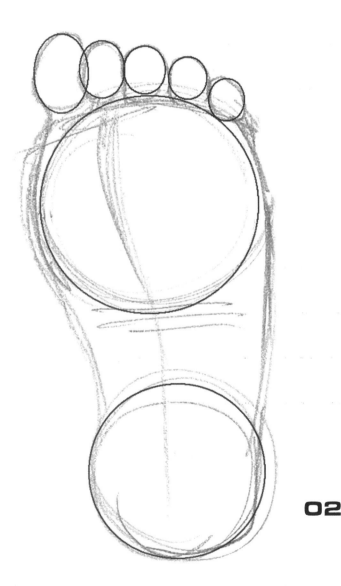

02

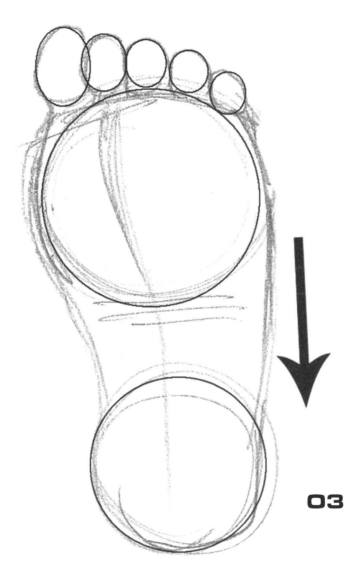

03

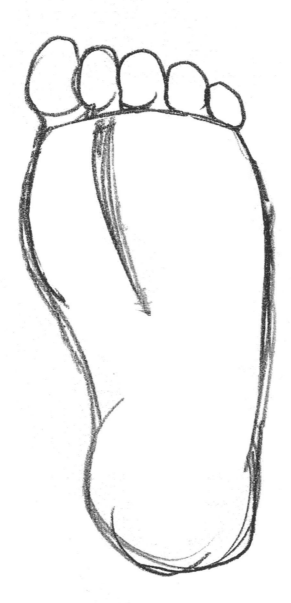

Hands and Feet

Here's the foot like you'd typically see it. Notice the circles for the ba
and heel are still there, but they're drawn in perspective to reflect the
pose. The new addition is the circle drawn in for the ankle. This will
help you figure out the connection for the rest of the leg. All the step
remain the same as in the last example except the toes. The toes w
look more like cylinders, so approach drawing them that way.

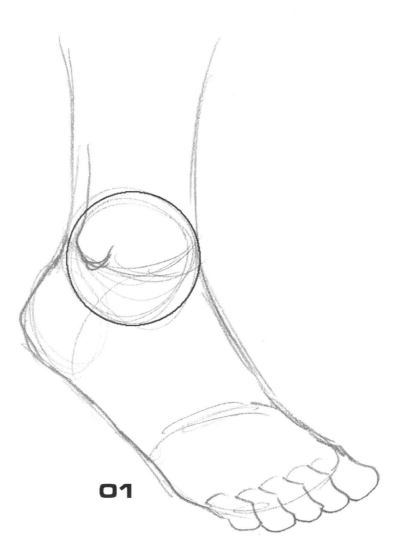

01

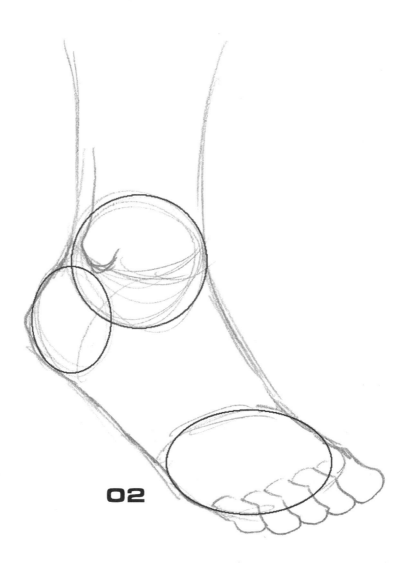

02

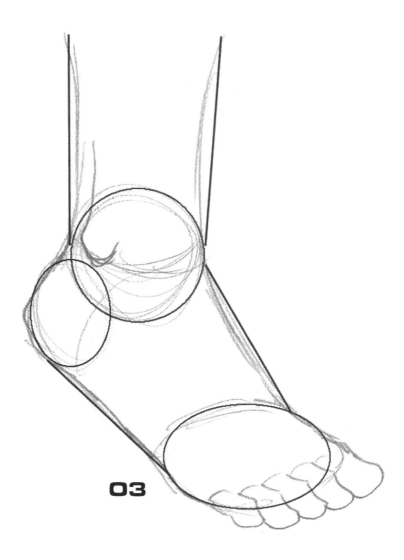

03

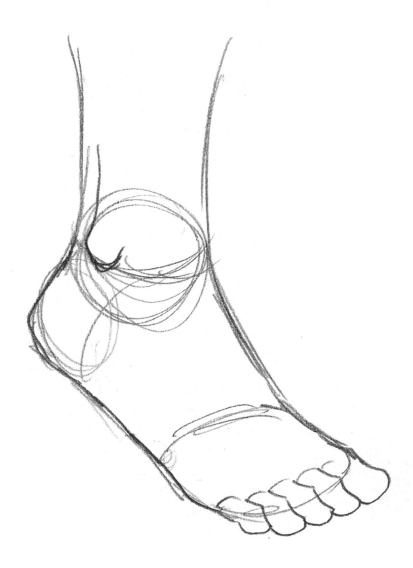

Hands and Feet

Drawing the foot from the rear gets even more complicated due to the fact that the Achilles tendon is smack in the middle of the body part. When you break it down, all it is is a pair of triangles that touch at their tips. It's probably gonna be tough to look at your own foot from this angle, so get someone to pose for you or take a picture.

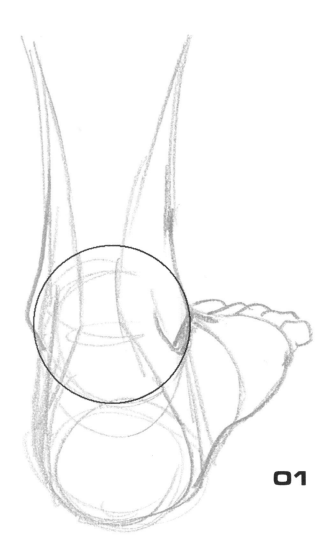

01

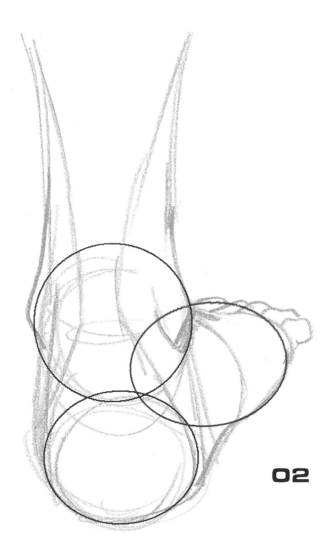

02

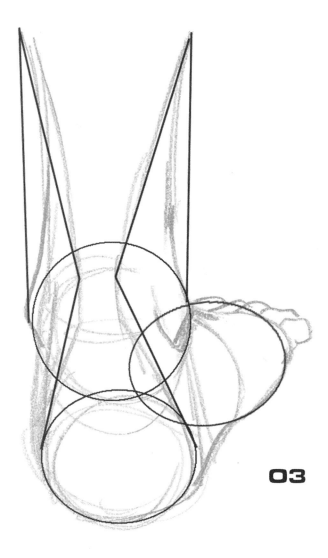

03

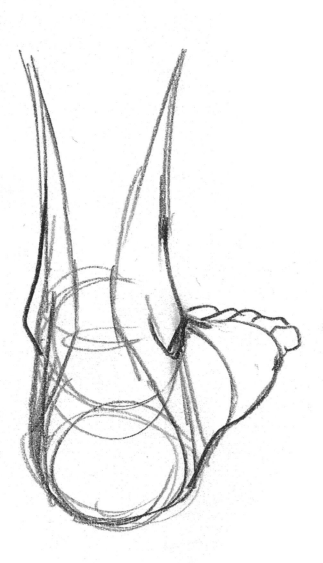

Hands and Feet

Here're the feet and legs in action. When you're laying out the figure, the feet will generally be small ovals at the ends of the legs, but there will be times when it'll be necessary to draw in those little piggies. So, like the saying says, "there's no time like the present" to start understanding how to draw feet without the socks or shoes. Understanding now will make your drawing skill that much stronger.

Articulation

You will hear the term "points of articulation" used frequently in this book and in many other situations, especially when discussing figures in movement. A point of articulation is the point that controls movement of a portion of the body. It is important to know where the articulation points are and how they behave in order to draw characters with realistic and believable movement.

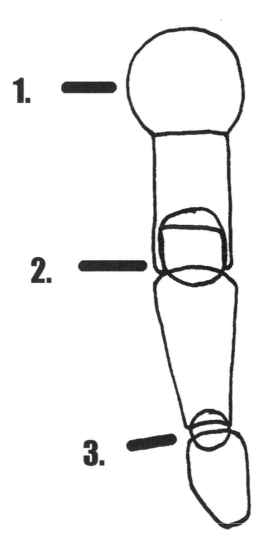

1. —

2. —

3. —

In this simple drawing of an arm, the points of articulation are marked with circles. This means that you have three places you can determine the pose of the arm at.

Articulation

Along with knowing where the points of articulation are, it is a good idea to know how they behave. Luckily, we have our own bodies to use as reference.

For example, your elbow only bends in one direction, but your wrist and shoulder have a much greater range of motion.

103

Articulation

So let us get into articulation a bit more. On this model, you will see more points of articulation. The human body has tons of them; you have 18 on each arm alone. When setting up your figures, you need to consider the big ones and work your way down to the smaller ones.

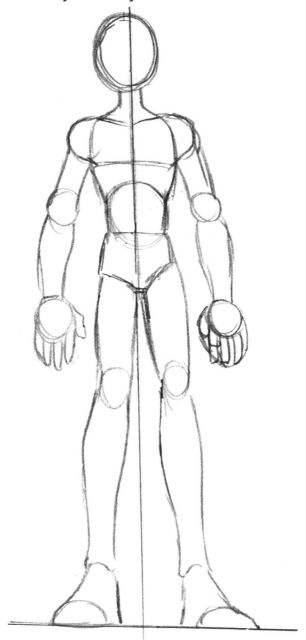

104

Articulation

We've already touched on the arms. The other three major areas are the head, torso, and legs. Getting these three areas right in your basic sketch is key.

Articulation

Once you've finished this, you can start to add details to your figure, and tha is when you consider the other points of articulation, like the fingers and toe

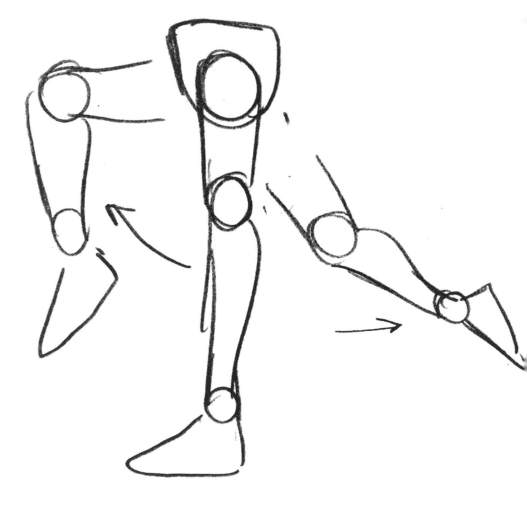

Drawing The Figure

The main character of most Shonen manga and usually a big player in many Shoujo is the average male. Modest of build and height, this body type is one that you will be hard pressed to avoid using. Even if the style you choose to draw in is slightly different, the proportions on your average male character will follow this basic form!

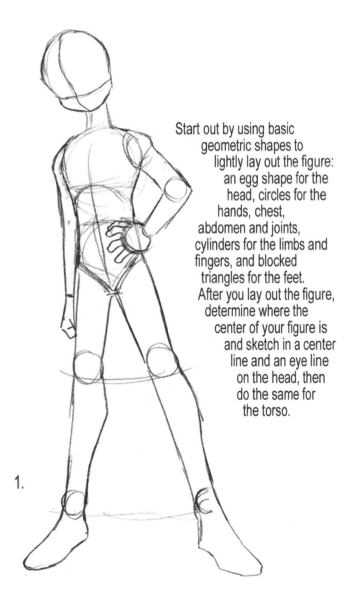

Start out by using basic geometric shapes to lightly lay out the figure: an egg shape for the head, circles for the hands, chest, abdomen and joints, cylinders for the limbs and fingers, and blocked triangles for the feet. After you lay out the figure, determine where the center of your figure is and sketch in a center line and an eye line on the head, then do the same for the torso.

1.

Drawing The Figure

2.

Drawing The Figure

Using the guidelines that you drew on the head, draw eyes, the ear, nose, and mouth.

When drawing hair, keep in mind that the hair rests slightly above the skull, so leave a little room so it rests naturally on the head. In manga, be sure to treat the hair as one whole mass, not several strands of hair. As you build hair, keep in mind the way real hair grows to help you determine the hair shape.

3.

Drawing The Figure

Here's why you were supposed to draw lightly— now we get to add the costume. Remember, clothes don't fit right up against the body (unless you're wearing spandex or a body stocking). Allow a bit of room between the body and clothing. Use the layout figure as a guide. A good idea is to take a look at yourself in a mirror wearing something similar to your character's clothes and standing in the same pose to get the folds, wrinkles, and details right.

4.

110

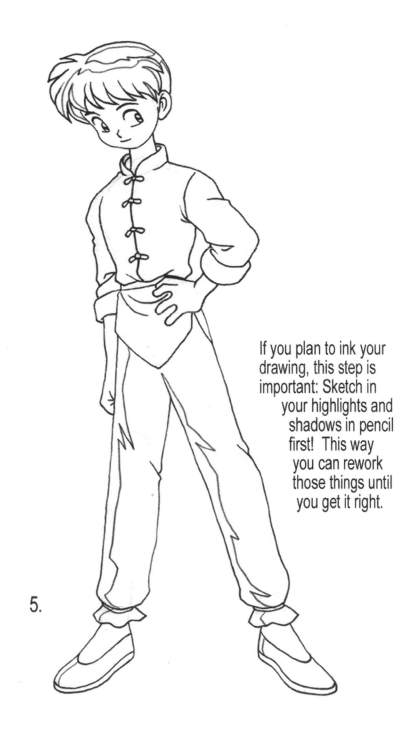

5.

If you plan to ink your drawing, this step is important: Sketch in your highlights and shadows in pencil first! This way you can rework those things until you get it right.

Drawing The Figure

You've got your illustration perfect. Now you ink it in! This last step is where you can add textures, freckles, or things that you think up on the fly, and you're done.

6.

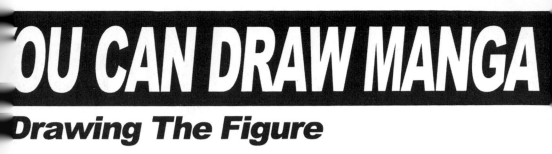

Drawing The Figure

There are distinct differences between the male and female form, although in manga today, especially shoujo manga, those differences are intentionally minimized or completely disregarded.

The two major areas of difference between male and female are the chest and the hips. On males, the chest is larger and more barrel-shaped. In comparison, the female chest is more oval and tapers down.

⟵ The main difference is this line. ⟶

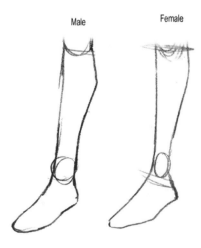

Male   Female

113

YOU CAN DRAW MANGA

Drawing The Figure

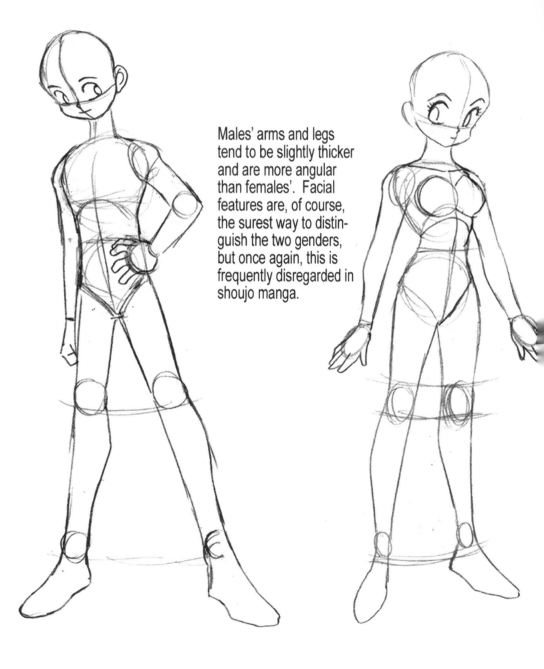

Males' arms and legs tend to be slightly thicker and are more angular than females'. Facial features are, of course, the surest way to distinguish the two genders, but once again, this is frequently disregarded in shoujo manga.

Drawing The Figure

As mentioned on the previous page, there are distinct differences between the male and female form, but the process is still the same. So, let's begin with the layout.

Follow step 1 from the male figure, remembering that the female torso tapers in the middle, giving the hourglass shape. Also, keep the limbs lean and curvy rather than thick and angular.

1.

Drawing The Figure

Again, using guide-lines, layout the facial features. Giving the hint of eyelashes is a great way to add that touch of femininity. Using guidelines in the chest will help properly position the breasts.

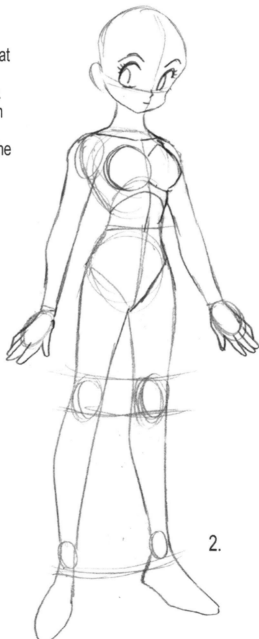

2.

Drawing The Figure

It's time for the hair. This time, instead of just one hair shape, now you've got two, so be sure to treat them as such, not as one whole mass.

3.

Drawing The Figure

Clothes on females will generally fit a little more snugly than on males, but always keep in mind of the types of costumes they have on and draw accordingly.

4.

Drawing The Figure

Lay out your
shadows and
highlights in
pencil.

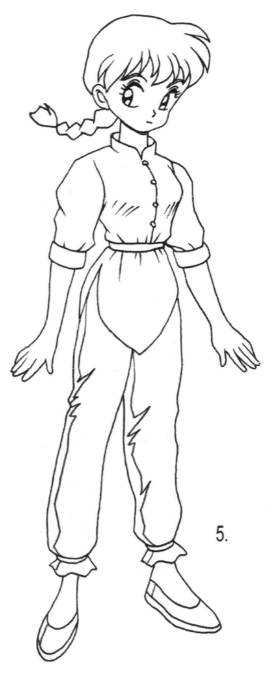

5.

Drawing The Figure

There is nothing wrong with emulating your favorite manga—in fact, I quite encourage it. In Japan, it is institutionally nurtured through the apprentice system, which has young artists working under the supervision of more experienced masters.

Ink and go!

6.

Drawing The Figure

Drawing adult characters is fairly straightforward. The major difference between these figures and the previous younger ones is that their limbs are longer and their heads are slightly smaller. This makes them slightly more proportionally balanced than younger characters, probably since they have grown out of puberty.

Drawing The Figure

Of course not every character you are going to draw will be a young, teen to twenty-something male or female. You may even want to create a manga aimed at a more mature audience, and then you will definitely need adult characters.

You will be pretty hard pressed to tell a story without any adults, although it has been done, so take the time to learn the small alterations you need to make to create believable adults. The same body differences between males and females still apply.

Drawing The Figure

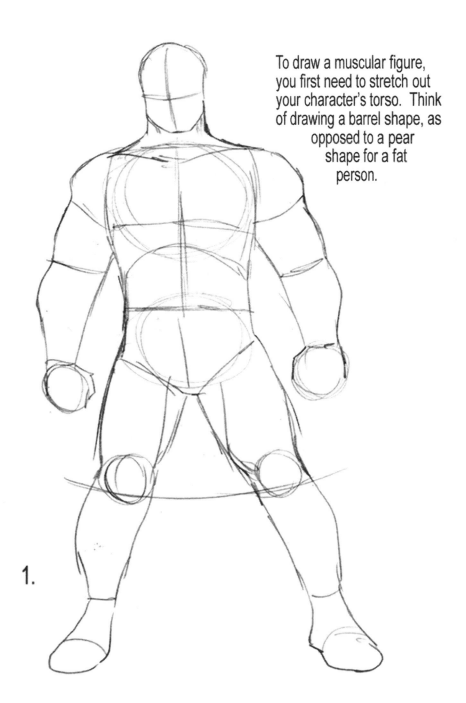

To draw a muscular figure, you first need to stretch out your character's torso. Think of drawing a barrel shape, as opposed to a pear shape for a fat person.

1.

Drawing The Figure

Then exaggerate all the muscles that you normally draw by broadening them.

2.

Drawing The Figure

You can also make a character appear more muscular by drawing them in tight clothing.

3.

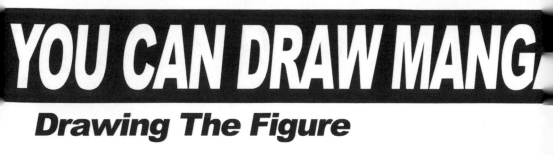

Drawing The Figure

In American comics, this is the most common body type, the muscular male. In manga, it is uncommon, and when it is used, you are almost always dealing with someone who is an antagonist, usually a bully.

Even in manga that revolve around hand-to-hand combat, the overly muscular form is not one that is idolized. Instead, the idealized male form in most manga is a body that has a balance between strength, flexibility and dexterity.

4.

Drawing The Figure

Manga does an incredible job of reflecting reality and all its facets, and in the real world, not everyone is slim and trim. Even if none of your main characters are overweight, you will want to learn how to draw this body type so you can create variety in your background figures.

All the same figure-drawing rules apply, though since you are drawing an overweight person, the overweight body-shape will fall more into a pear shape than a rectangle.

Drawing The Figure

Remember that it is not enough to simply draw a large belly on a figure to make it fat.

Drawing The Figure

When a person gains
weight, they gain it all over
their body, and you will
want to make sure that
your figure is balanced by
spreading the weight
around evenly.

YOU CAN DRAW MANGA

Drawing The Figure

Men and woman gain weight differently, with men tending to carry a lot of weight around their midriffs. In contrast, women often gain weight in their thighs and breasts as well as their midriffs. If you are not certain how a person will look, use reference. In fact, use reference as often as possible!

Drawing The Figure

The old man may be the most versatile character in fantastic fiction. The archetype that immediately springs to mind the is lecherous old man, but there are so many others. The old man who sends the young heroes on a mission, the old man who leads the heroes on a quest, the patriarch of the family whom the hero is trying to please, and the curmudgeon with whom the hero has to put up are just a few of the examples of what this body type is used for, so I hope you have mastered it.

This body type is more slender or even wizened. Stoop the back over and bend all the limbs.

1.

Drawing The Figure

If you are going to lean an older man against a cane, make sure that you ha enough bend in the arms and body to give the lean a sense of weight.

Drawing The Figure

Then go on and add some wrinkles. It can be as simple as some lines on the forehead or as involved as complex tracery all over the face.

3.

YOU CAN DRAW MANGA

Drawing The Figure

4.

Drawing The Figure

he number of manga that contain
andfather-and grandmother-type
haracters is considerable, and the
number of roles they fill equally
merous. Just like the grandfather,
e grandmother-or, more precisely,
he old woman body type-can be
perfectly suited to the role of old,
cherous comic relief. On the other
de of the coin, old women can be
uturers who are there to provide
advice and progress the story
through revelatory exposition.

1.

Drawing The Figure

2.

Drawing The Figure

3.

Drawing The Figure

4.

Drawing The Figure

The short stature of this body type makes the character seem frail and older. A good rule of thumb is the shorter and the more wrinkly the character, the older (s)he is.

Drawing The Figure

These basic body types are all you will need to make great manga. There are a few others you might want to use, but for your basic stories, you have all you need here. I hope you have begun to get comfortable with these body types, because we are going to be moving ahead full steam from here.

Character Design

One of the most fun and also most difficult things in manga is character design. The main reason why is probably because it's really hard to come up with something new that hasn't been seen before. Now that doesn't mean that we, as artists, can't draw our inspiration from other things. In this chapter, we will go over using reference and costume design and how these elements help in developing memorable and, hope-fully, original characters. Let's get started!

Character Design

Let's warm up with some basics. Remember, when starting an illustration, make sure you lay out the figure using basic shapes.

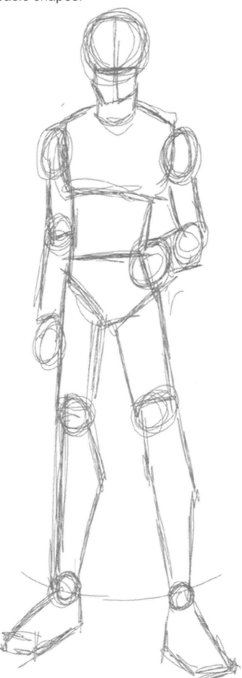

Character Design

Then, lightly sketch in the details. Keep in mind that when you draw clothes, make sure that you are including the wrinkles and folds. These details will help not only give the audience an accurate image of the type of clothes the character is wearing, they will also help make your illustration look solid and three-dimensional. In designing characters, personality is a huge factor in what a character wears, how they stand, and how they look overall.

YOU CAN DRAW MANGA

Character Design

YOU CAN DRAW MANGA

Character Design

Dark colors, and most importantly blacks, send the quickest message to the viewer. When illustrating in blacks, be sure to lay out your highlights in pencil before you go to the inking stage.

Character Design

Okay, let's design a futuristic space warrior. We start with a pose that would compliment this character: rigid with a wide, balanced stance.

OU CAN DRAW MANGA

haracter Design

YOU CAN DRAW MANGA

Character Design

Now we need to choose a look for his wardrobe. A good place to start is with uniforms and equipment used by police and soldiers today—in this instance, a helmet, chest armor, and, of course, his pistol.

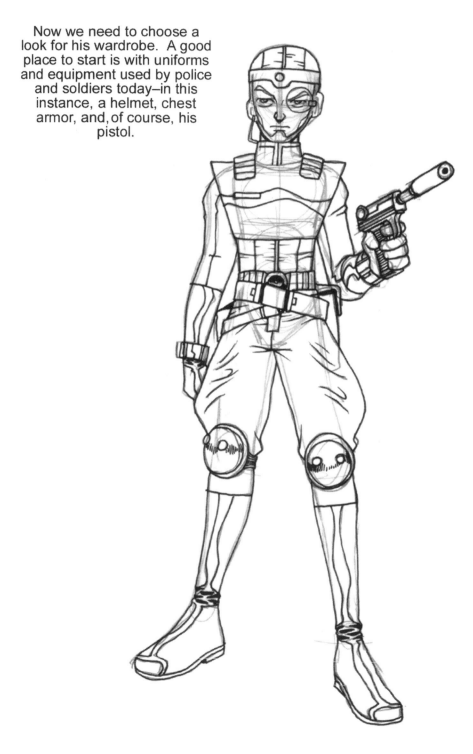

Character Design

As you can see, several present-day elements can be used to influence your futuristic designs. S.W.A.T. team uniforms as well as some older elements were used as a jumping-off point for this design.

Character Design

The design goes a step beyond the inital S.W.A.T. uniform but still keeps some of the same older uniform elements, incorporating these pieces in your design will help keep the uniform believable.

When drawing armor, be sure to draw the armor fitting properly onto the figure. Armor won't sit right against the form, you need to account for the muscles, skin, and clothing under the armor.

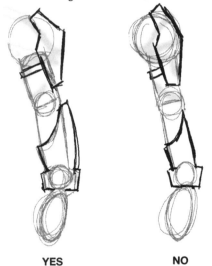

YES   **NO**

And as mentioned before, always try to use reference when you can. It is the easiest and fastest way to get the results you want.

YOU CAN DRAW MANGA
Character Design

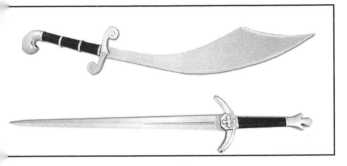

Coming up with new ideas for weapons is again found in the old. Using old swords has helped in coming up with the design for this adventurer's weapon of choice.

Character design isn't only about who they are or what they wear, it's also about things they come in contact with. Accessories and weapons your character uses can speak volumes about who they are and where they've come from.

There's a certian romantic quality about having swords for weapons, swords are a popular weapon for heros in many stories.

151

Character Design

Hairstyles are great ways to add personality to a character. The semi-afro is a popular hairstyle coming back into the mainstream, and besides it's fun to draw!

Photo reference is not only a starting off point but can be also used as an exact piece of the character's wardrobe. Using reference will always help you get a better drawing as well as help you become a better artist.

Basketball sneakers have a certain "look" to them, such as the tounge flap sticking out or fat laces.

Clothes don't always make the man. When designing characters, body type also says a lot about a character. In the case of these two guys, they're wearing the same outfits, but they are built differently. What personality are you getting from each of them?

The baseball cap is a favorite among the "rebel" types.

Character Design

A raised hood, a hat, and sunglasses all cover this character's face. Design elements that create a barrier between the character and the world can indicate many things, like a desire to go unnoticed.

Character Design

One of the most successful subgenera of science fiction is that of space battles, usually involving space armadas, space fighters, and often space-worthy robots. The most important element of design in stories like this is how the uniform will look, since most of the characters will be wearing the same thing. You may differentiate between different military divisions and jobs, but the overall design of the uniform is very significant.

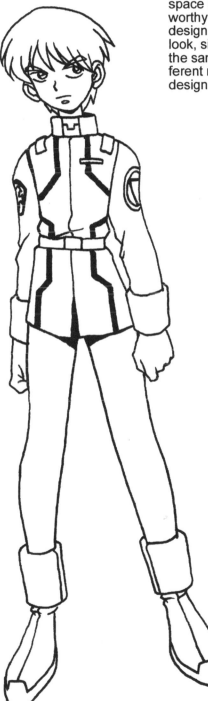

A few things that are important on any uniform: what side you're on (the shoulder insignia), who you are (a name tag on the chest), and what your rank is (shoulder tabs).

155

YOU CAN DRAW MANGA

Character Design

The "Rogue Type" character here is wearing high boots, a midriff shirt, and high-cut jacket all complete the roguish look.

The skin-tight outfit is not quite as easy as it may seem. The real trick to it is laying out the highlights on the outfit. A good place to look to for reference is real life. Find a highly reflective material like a shiny plastic cup or patent leather shoes so you can study what light does when it hits it.

YOU CAN DRAW MANGA
Character Design

The all-black leather outfit is a very popular costume for "edgy" heroines.

YOU CAN DRAW MANGA

Character Design

There are many different types of uniforms that people wear. Look around you and see how people are dressing, and then fast-forward them a couple hundred years.

Adding gloves and boots generally helps enhance a futuristic character's look.

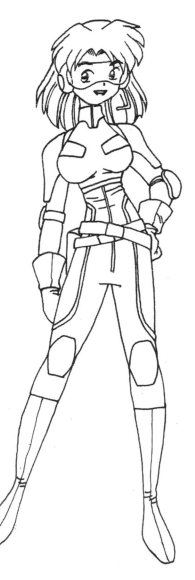

These designs are relatively the same, with just minor differences. As you can see, with small additions and subtractions, there can be several variations on the same line of thinking.

Character Design

Drawing cloth properly is almost as important as the figure itself. In this example, you want to treat the cape as a separate shape, almost as a separate character. This approach will help make it easier to draw more convincing capes and clothing.

Character Design

Character Design

Here is an example of lots of cloth. Don't let that affect how you draw your figure. Always start with a light sketch using basic shapes. Then, as you go to the drawing of clothes, remember to draw the clothes flowing around the figure, not clinging to it.

Character Design

The tiara signifies royalty, a must for a space princess!

The long, slender pistol reflects the character's slender build.

Drawing Villains

Now that you've mastered the basics of drawing and you've been practicing with designing your own heroic characters, it's time to have a little fun. The Bad Guys! Ya love to hate 'em, now let's give designing 'em a try! As you'll see, inspiraion for the bad guys can come from many different people, places and things. Sometimes, even your worst nightmare can be the *best* source for your sinister sketckbook scaries!

So, let's get started!!

Drawing Villains

Let's start with our grumpy pal from the last page.

As always, you want to start every figure with the basic shapes. The proportions of this guy are that of a body-builder.

When you draw the body-builder-type body, here's a basic tip to make it easier: Draw the chest twice as wide as the hips.

Drawing Villains

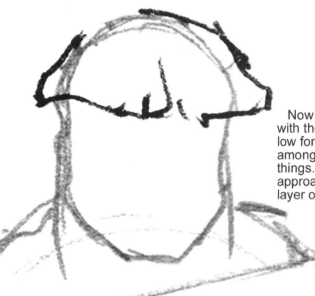

Now you want to evil him up! Starting with the head, we'll give him the traditional low forehead and large brow common among the demons who just like to break things. When drawing this feature, approach it as if you were applying a new layer on top of your basic figure.

Next we're gonna add the two things that 'll make your drawing a demon: pointed ears d horns. These features are essentially angles, and placement of the horns is really to you. Do a little research on horned imals. Where do they keep theirs?

171

Drawing Villains

Ears, horns and forehead are done, but we're not through yet!

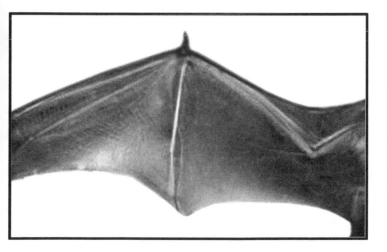

Here's another instance where using reference will help make your drawing realistic and believable. Basing your creations on things that exist in nature is a sure way to attain a believability you wouldn't get otherwise.

Pay close attention to why things are the way they are, not just how they look. For instance, the bones of the bat wing stretch the loose skin for flight, and if you notice, the bones all meet at one point on the wing.

Drawing Villains

Wings usually attach on or just above the shoulder blades of most upright, walking characters.

Also, the time's come for the eyes, mouth and tail. Sometimes, eyes without pupils are scarier than with. Experiment—it's your drawing!

Drawing Villains

Time for details and textures! Details like black around the eyes, hair and claws are nice touches that will add even more menace to an already formidable agent of evil! And textures like those found on the tail and the skin of the wings break up empty space on your character and also give a little depth and form.

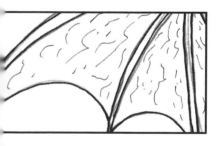

Drawing Villains

And ther you go! A full
demon ready to wreak havoc
on all things good..
Evil sold separately...

Drawing Villains

What a difference a power tool makes! As shown here, reference has a lot to do with making or breaking this drawing. Getting the hands and arms positioned correctly would be difficult, even for the seasoned artist.

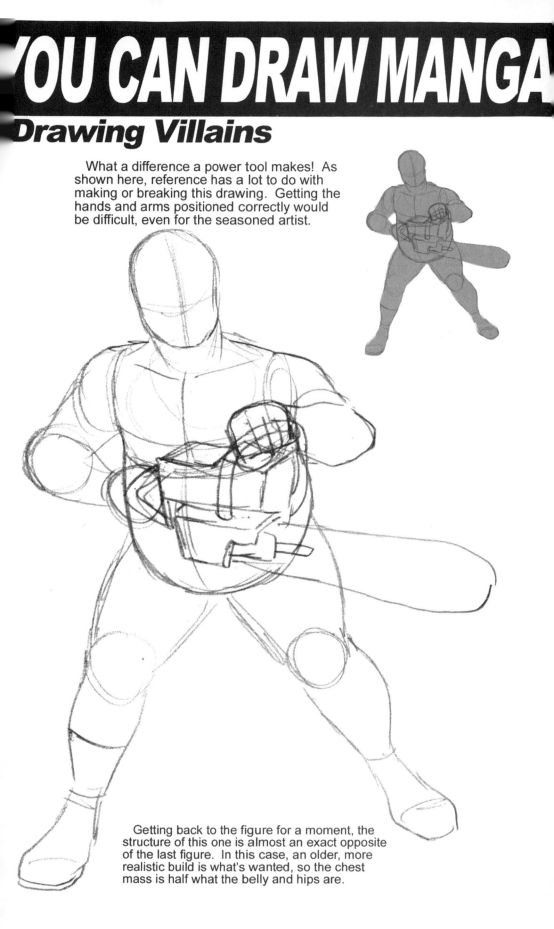

Getting back to the figure for a moment, the structure of this one is almost an exact opposite of the last figure. In this case, an older, more realistic build is what's wanted, so the chest mass is half what the belly and hips are.

177

YOU CAN DRAW MANGA

Drawing Villains

The evil is in the details!
So use the 'Ref'!

Drawing Villains

It's time for the simple little details, like arm hair and splatters of stuff that is hopefully tree sap. Also, you can use this step to clean up your pencil lines.

Cloth is harder to draw than it looks, especially draped cloth. This is another opportunity to use the almighty reference!

179

Now just fill in the blacks when you go to ink, and this guy is all finished. When you are inking, don't forget to erase your pencil lines!

Drawing Villains

Let's take the heavy-set figure from the last section and try something different. Remember that the mass of the chest is smaller than the hips and belly.

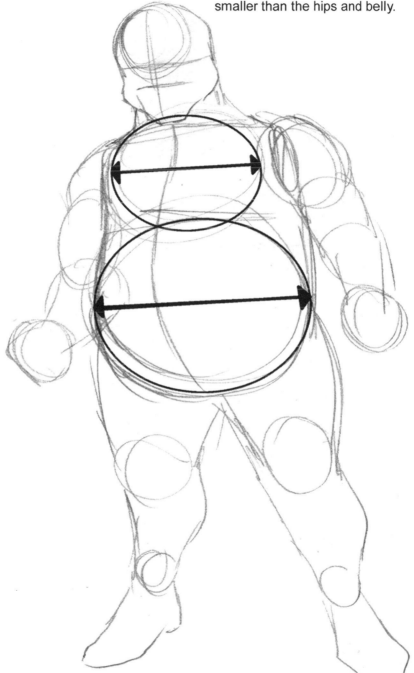

Drawing Villains

By simply adding a single element, it completely changes the direction the development of the character takes. Look at this sketch. What do you think this person could be?

Drawing Villains

In many cases, figuring out the face can be one of the best ways to create a great character. Most artists will agree that if you can come up with a great face, the rest will fall into place. Here, the goatee, Fu Manchu mustache and missing eye already suggest a personality.

Drawing Villains

Looks like the "ayes" have it! Details like the hat and coat say "pirate," but the laser-eye and robotic arm and peg-leg tell what time period he plunders in. Mixing elements from other time periods can make for interesting combinations.

Drawing Villains

Tighten up your pencil work and lay out your highlights.

185

Drawing Villains

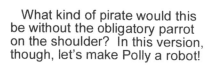

What kind of pirate would this be without the obligatory parrot on the shoulder? In this version, though, let's make Polly a robot!

Weapons

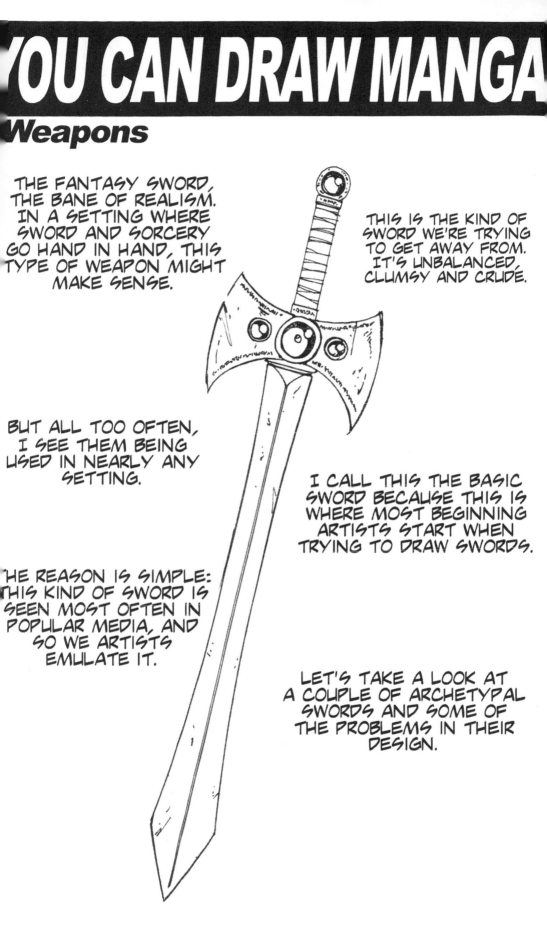

THE FANTASY SWORD, THE BANE OF REALISM. IN A SETTING WHERE SWORD AND SORCERY GO HAND IN HAND, THIS TYPE OF WEAPON MIGHT MAKE SENSE.

THIS IS THE KIND OF SWORD WE'RE TRYING TO GET AWAY FROM. IT'S UNBALANCED, CLUMSY AND CRUDE.

BUT ALL TOO OFTEN, I SEE THEM BEING USED IN NEARLY ANY SETTING.

I CALL THIS THE BASIC SWORD BECAUSE THIS IS WHERE MOST BEGINNING ARTISTS START WHEN TRYING TO DRAW SWORDS.

THE REASON IS SIMPLE: THIS KIND OF SWORD IS SEEN MOST OFTEN IN POPULAR MEDIA, AND SO WE ARTISTS EMULATE IT.

LET'S TAKE A LOOK AT A COUPLE OF ARCHETYPAL SWORDS AND SOME OF THE PROBLEMS IN THEIR DESIGN.

187

Weapons

HERE ARE TWO WEAPONS IN THE SERVICE OF GOOD AND EVIL, RESPECTIVELY. NO ONE WOULD EVER USE THE SWORDS UNLESS THEY HAD NO OTHER CHOICE. THESE ARE STRICTLY ORNAMENTS--FOR SHOW, NOT USE. THE BLADES ARE FAR TOO LARGE AND CUMBERSOME TO BE USEFUL. LARGE HILTS COVERED WITH SKULLS OR ENCRUSTED WITH PRECIOUS JEWELS ONLY GET IN THE WAY AND INJURE THE PERSON USING THE SWORD. STILL, THEY LOOK KINDA COOL!

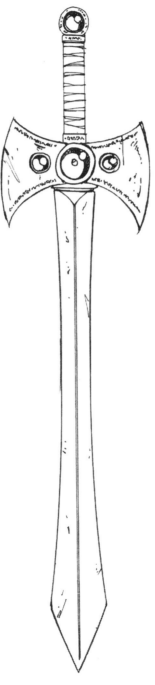

Weapons

NOW, THESE SWORDS MAKE A LITTLE MORE SENSE. YOU CAN DRAW THEM FROM THEIR SHEATHS WITHOUT SEVERELY INJURING YOURSELF. HERE FORM FOLLOWS FUNCTION, AND WE'RE NOT RIPPING OFF THE SWORD OF OMENS. I THINK ONE OF THE MAIN PROBLEMS ARTISTS HAVE WHEN STARTING OUT IS A LACK OF UNDERSTANDING ABOUT THEIR SUBJECT. IN THE SAME WAY YOU CAN BENEFIT FROM A BETTER UNDERSTANDING OF THE HUMAN BODY, YOU TRY TO FIND OUT A LITTLE ABOUT THE WEAPONS YOU MIGHT TRY TO DEPICT.

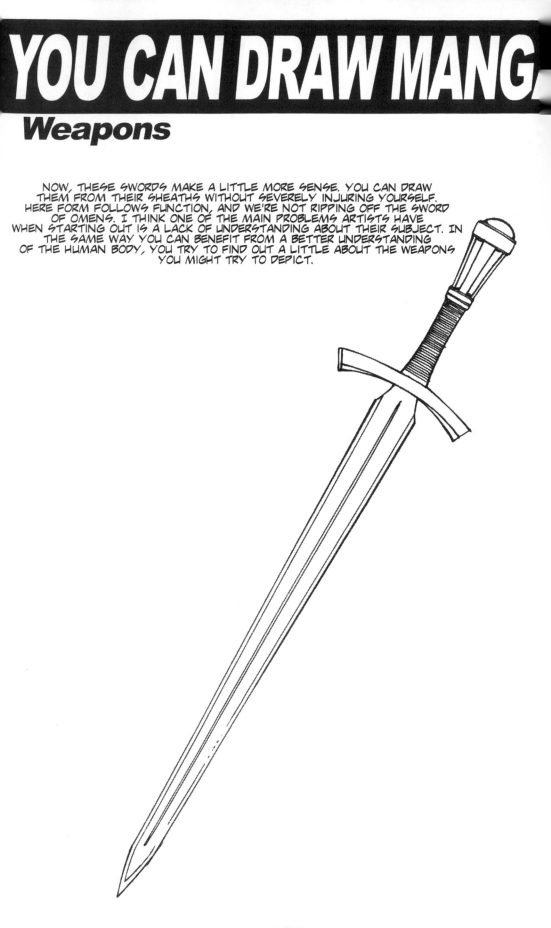

Weapons

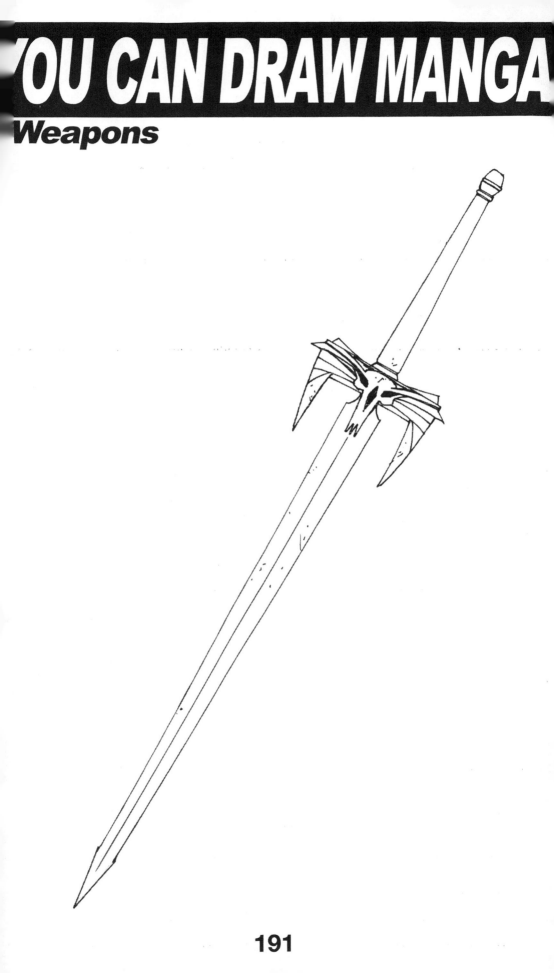

Weapons

LET'S TAKE A LOOK AT THE ANATOMY OF A SWORD. ALMOST ALL SWORDS SHARE A SIMILAR CONSTRUCTION AND DESIGN. I'VE LABELED THE MOST BASIC PARTS FOR MOST SWORDS.

HERE IS A DESCRIPTION OF THE BASIC PARTS AND SOME OF THE REASONING BEHIND THEM.

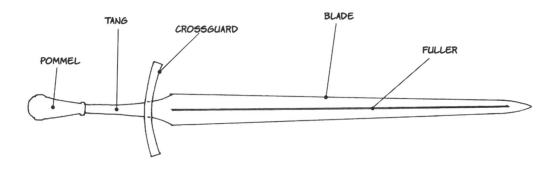

THE BLADE:
THE MOST USED PART OF THE WEAPON, MORE TIME IS PUT INTO DESIGNING THE MOST EFFECTIVE BLADE POSSIBLE. THE BLADE CAN BE DESIGNED FOR MOST ANY PURPOSE: CHOPPING, PIERCING, SLASHING, SAWING, OR HANGING ON A WALL. THEY ARE ALSO MADE TO FIT INTO CERTAIN STYLES OF FIGHTING.

THE FULLER:
KNOWN MORE OFTEN AS THE BLOODGROOVE, THE FULLER IS A WEDGE-SHAPED GROOVE THAT FOLLOWS THE LENGTH OF THE SWORD. WHEN THE OPPONENT IS STABBED WITH THE SWORD, A VACUUM MAY CLOSE AROUND THE BLADE, MAKING IT NEARLY IMPOSSIBLE TO PULL THE WEAPON OUT AGAIN. THE FULLER CHANNELS BLOOD FROM THE WOUND, MAKING IT EASIER TO WITHDRAW THE SWORD.

THE TANG:
THE TANG IS THE PART OF THE SWORD THAT CONTINUES DOWN PAST THE HILT AND INTO THE HANDLE. SOME TANGS CONTINUE AS ONE PIECE TO BECOME THE POMMEL.

Weapons

THE HILT OR CROSSGUARD:
MEANT TO HELP BLOCK THE BLOW FROM A SWORD. IT ALSO PROTECTS THE
HANDS FROM BEING INJURED IN BATTLE. DEPENDING ON THE DESIGN, IT
CAN ALSO BE USED TO TRAP AN OPPONENT'S SWORD OR TO HELP DISARM
THE OPPONENT.

CROSSGUARD

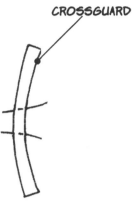

THE HANDLE AND GRIP:
THE HANDLE IS TYPICALLY MADE OF WOOD, THOUGH HORN AND OTHER
MATERIALS ARE USED. THE HANDLE SURROUNDS THE TANG AND MAY BE
FASTENED BY BOLTS OR CORD. THE GRIP IS
USUALLY LEATHER OR CORD.

POMMEL

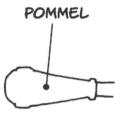

THE POMMEL:
THE POMMEL IS NOT JUST THERE TO REST YOUR HAND ON, IT'S MEANT TO
DELIVER DAMAGE. WHEN DRAWING THE SWORD, IT CAN BE USED TO STRIKE
THE HEAD AND CHEST OF THE OPPONENT. IN BATTLE, IT TAKES AWAY
THE ENEMY'S ABILITY TO USE A WEAPON BY SHATTERING BONES AND
DAMAGING MUSCLE TISSUE IN THE HANDS, ARM
AND SHOULDER.

Weapons

HERE ARE THE BASIC STEPS FOR DRAWING A STANDARD SWORD.

NOW LET'S TAKE A LOOK AT SOME DIFFERENT TYPES OF SWORDS AND SOME OF THE REASONS BEHIND THEIR DESIGN.

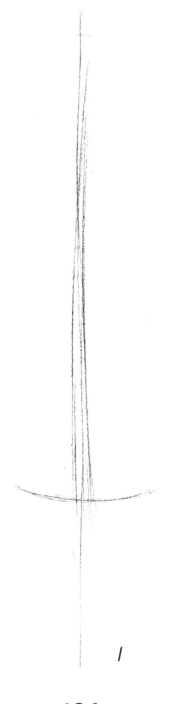

2

Weapons

ALSO KNOWN AS "THE NINJA SWORD", THE KATANA IS MADE FOR SMOOTH, FLUID MOVEMENT PRIMARILY A SLASHING WEAPON. WITH IT, AN EXPERT COULD CLEAVE AN ADULT MALE IN HALF WITH ONE BLOW. MANY OF THESE SWORDS ARE CONSIDERED WORKS OF ART. HERE I SHOW WHAT THE TANG OF THE BLADE LOOKS LIKE.

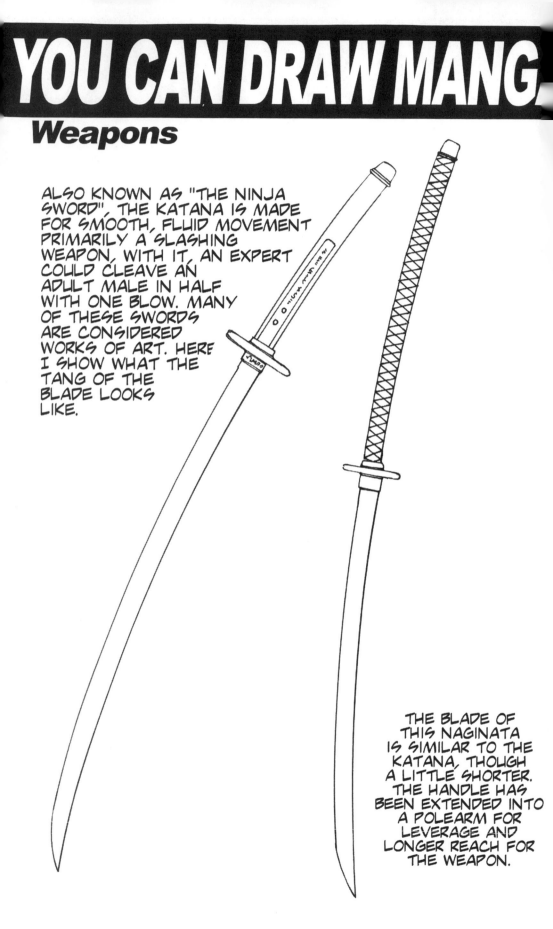

THE BLADE OF THIS NAGINATA IS SIMILAR TO THE KATANA, THOUGH A LITTLE SHORTER. THE HANDLE HAS BEEN EXTENDED INTO A POLEARM FOR LEVERAGE AND LONGER REACH FOR THE WEAPON.

YOU CAN DRAW MANGA

Weapons

LIGHT AND FLEXIBLE, THE RAPIER IS MADE TO STAB VITAL ORGANS WITH PRECISION. WITH PROPER SKILL, A SWORDSMAN CAN DEFEAT AN ARMOURED OPPONENT BY EXPLOITING WEAK SPOTS. SOME OF THESE SWORDS ARE SO WELL MADE THAT THEY CAN EVEN PIERCE THE ARMOUR ITSELF.

THIS IS AN EXECUTIONER'S SWORD. IT HAS NO POINT AND NO CROSSGUARD. IT'S MADE ONLY FOR CHOPPING HEADS. THE BLADE IS VERY HEAVY ON PURPOSE. THE BLADE IS DULL FROM USE AND POSSIBLY TO MAKE THE BEHEADING TAKE LONGER.

Weapons

LONG AND HEAVY, THE BASTARD SWORD IS MADE FOR SMASHING DOWN AN OPPONENT. WHILE EFFECTIVE, THESE SWORDS COULD ONLY BE USED BY THE MANLIEST OF MEN. THE SPIKES ON THE BLADE CAN BE USED CRACK AN ENEMY HELMET. THIS IS THE DOUBLE-HANDED VERSION, ONE OF MY FAVORITE SWORDS. IF YOU WANT TO SEE THIS SWORD IN USE, RENT A COPY OF "BRAVEHEART."

HERE ARE SOME OF THE SWORDS I'VE DESIGNED FROM LOOKING AT DIFFERENT SWORDS.

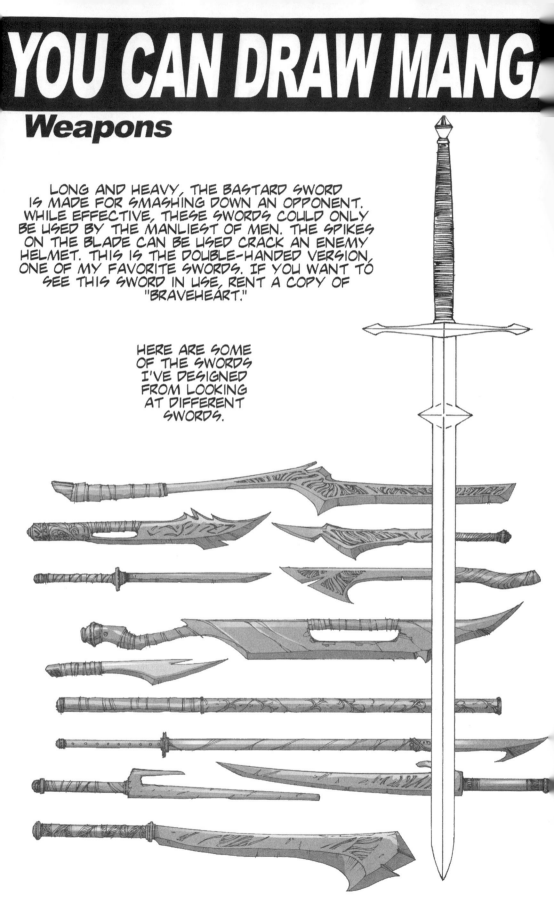

198

Weapons

To make your guns realisti-lookin, you must draw as much as possible from references. Futuristic guns are also based on present-day weapons. Slightly change certain features while retaining overall appearance is the key to making futuristic guns look real.

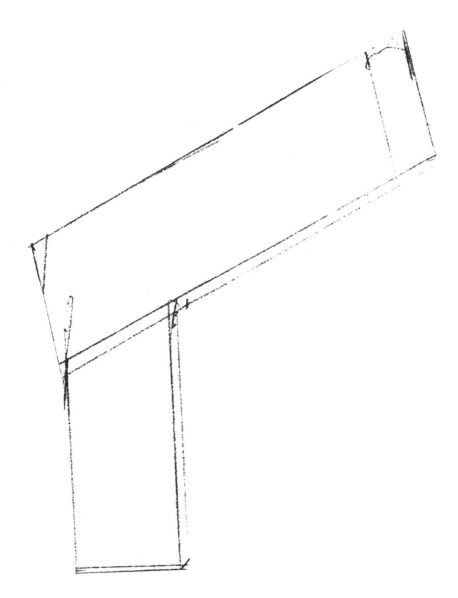

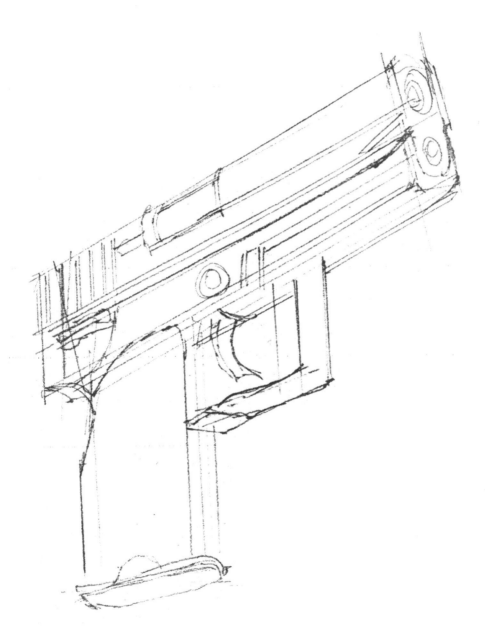

Weapons

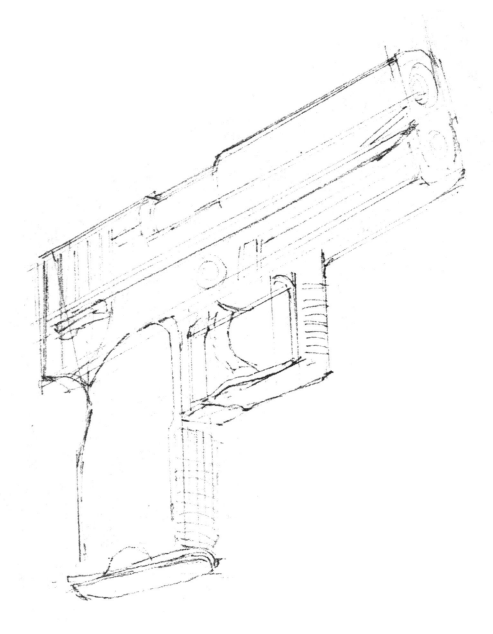

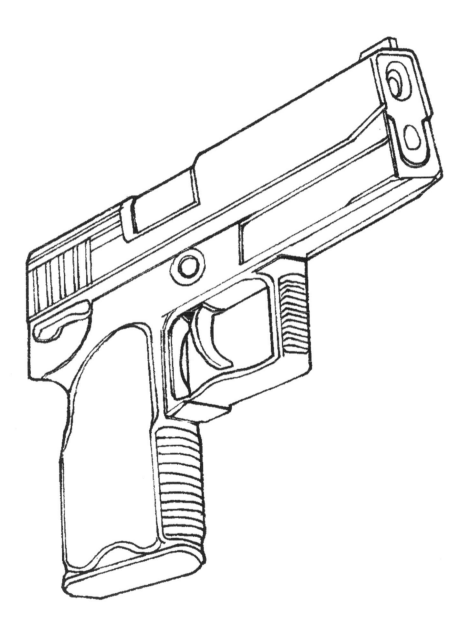

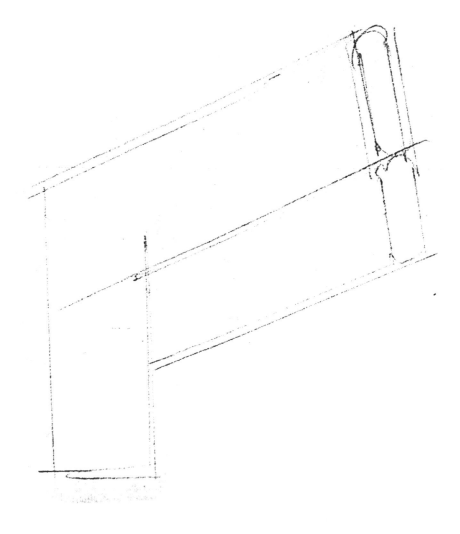

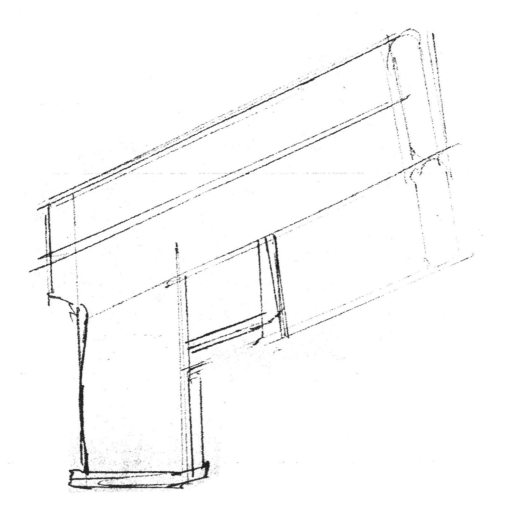

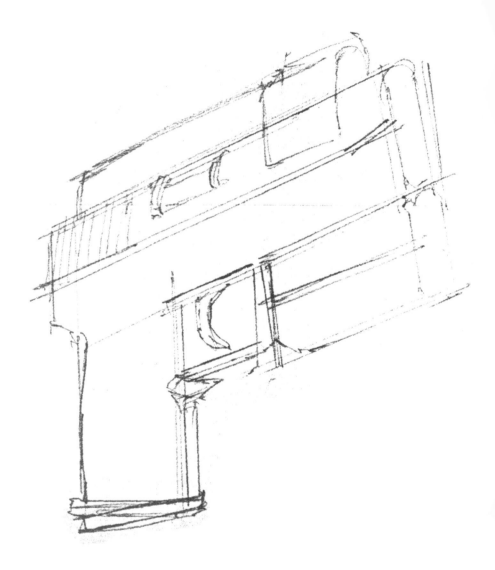

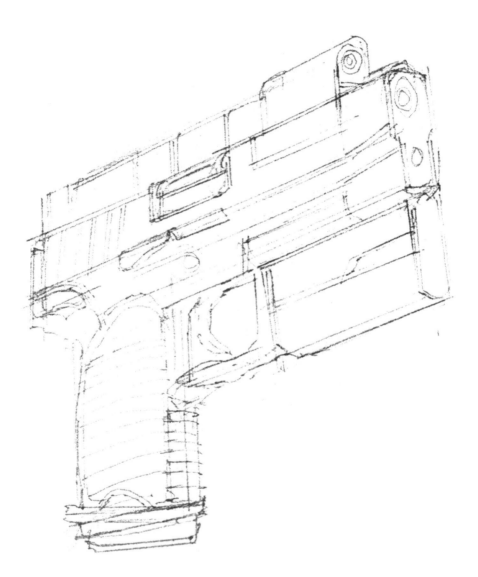

Weapons

Weapons

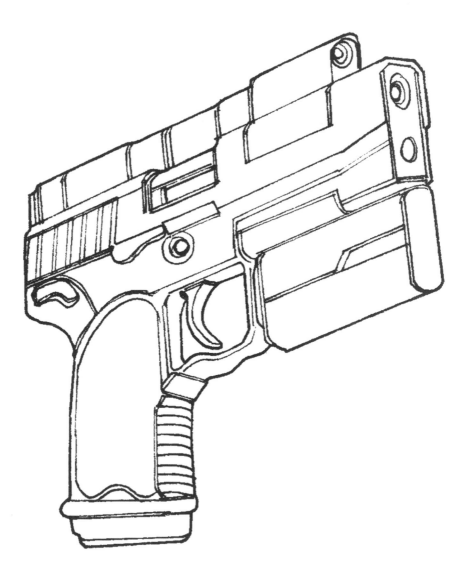

Weapons

The M16 Rifle is the standard weapon of choice of most military organizations in the world today. It is the symbol of Western might.

Here, we start off with the simplest of shapes--a box.

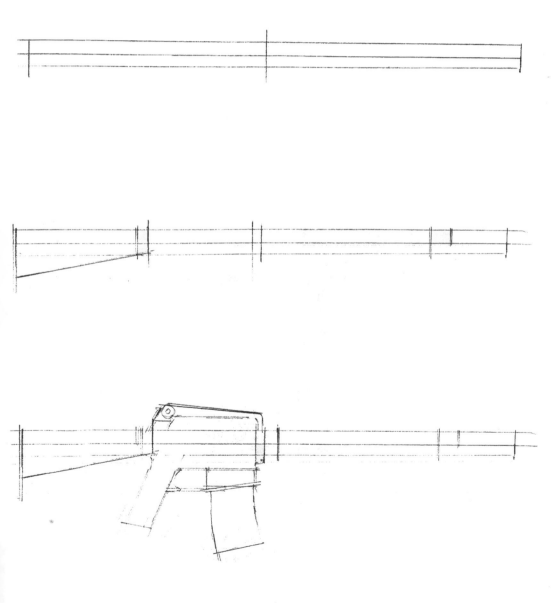

Weapons

Knowing how to draw guns from real life will help you draw realistic futuristic weapons later on. As with basic human anatom having a good working knowledge of how things work is the key to success.

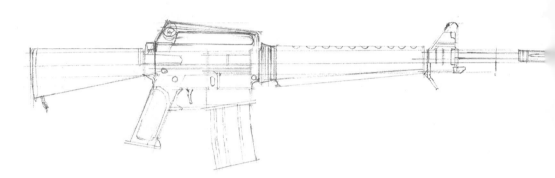

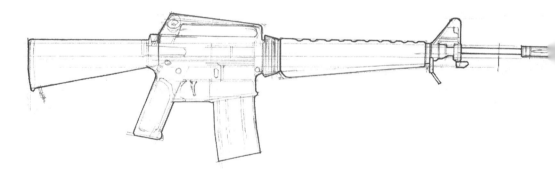

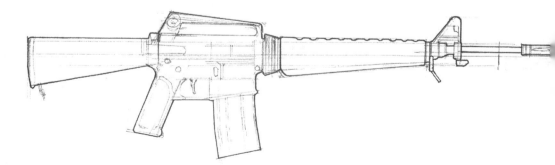

Weapons

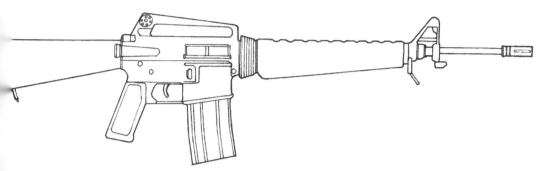

Adding a few trinkets makes this regular weapon look high tech while remaining very much believable.
This design is based on something I once saw in a movie: a regular M16 with a shotgun instead of the grenade launcher.
More and more equipment can be added to this.
The idea is to keep the basic familiar shape intact.

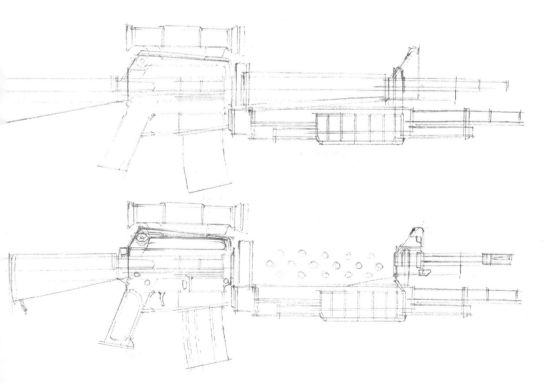

Weapons

Authors are encouraged to write about what they know.
There is a reason for this. Writing about things you
know firsthand makes your work more authentic.
Drawing comics is like writing. You have to know
what you are drawing.

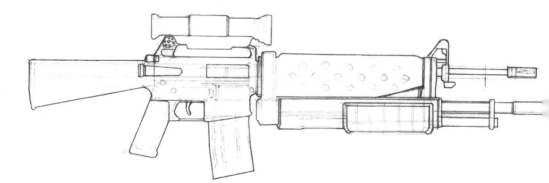

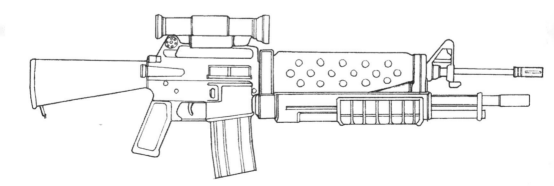

Weapons

In the end, there is still more and more to learn. This is what makes art so exciting. There is always a new horizon waiting to be explored. Just as you think you have mastered one thing, there is always another to be learned. Or perhaps we think we know all there is about one thing, only to find out we still have a long way to go. It takes a lifetime to master it all.

Human Monsters

This werewolf does a great job of tying the human and animal forms together. There is very little doubt that this creature is a wolf, and at the same time, you can look at it and clearly see that at one point it was a human and will probably take that form again soon.

Human Monsters

Some anthropomorphic monsters are easier than others. Cat people have the honor of being one of the easiest. All you really need to indicate a cat monster is a tail, some cat eyes, and whiskers, and you're off. If you want to go that extra step and show that you care, you can add some fur rendering and claws. People think cats are cuddly and cute, but werecats are to be feared more than werewolves. Cats are fickle and self-absorbed, liable to switch between kindness and cruelty in the blink of an eye. At least with a werewolf, you know what you are getting.

Human Monsters

Cat pupils are slitted, unlike round human pupils.

Cats are able to retract their claws back into their paws.

Human Monsters

Some people hypothesize that every creature has the genetic potential of every other creature locked away in its body. With a little genetic reforming, you might look like this. A fish/human hybrid will have a whole different set of problems and personality issues from the cat and wolf people. First, does a fishman need water every time he transforms? Can he breath air? The scary thing about a werefish is that his species has a lot to be upset about: A "small" amount of pollution in his ocean affects the delicate balance under the waves.

Webbed fingers help fishmen to move easily and quickly through water.

221

Human Monsters

A lot of transforming monsters fit very easily into stories about the environment. They can be seen as noble monsters defending the environment, but sometimes people transform themselves through science for selfish reasons. This insectman injected himself with an experimental formula that he hoped would allow him to make use of some of the positive aspects of insect life. Instead he ended up like this. He is understandably upset, and his new-found strength makes him a large threat.

Human Monsters

Some transforming monsters developed the ability to transform into human form as a way to hunt. This Black Widow Monster uses her human form to lure men to her lair, where she kills them and keeps them on wrap for later snacking. Arachnophobia is very common, and a good storyteller will exploit the fears of his readers to chill and thrill them.

Giant Monsters

Kaiju, or giant monsters, have their roots in the advent of the atomic age. Following the second World War, the cultural apprehension of the Japanese people concerning what atomic fallout might do to the world and the threat of the Cold War were expressed in films showcasing creatures that had often been created by radioactivity. The prevalence of radiation paranoia throughout the world, along with the high level of entertainment the films provided, made Giant Monster movies a global success, and their popularity continues to this day.

Giant Monsters

Just as Giant Monsters can be literally anything, you can tell a dizzying array of stories centered around a giant monster. Anything from a story of catastrophe to a romance can be effectively told in this sub-genre of monster movie. The freedom of Giant Monster stories is one of the things that makes them so much fun.

Giant Monsters

When creating a Giant Monster, there are four basic types to choose from: Quadrupedal, Arthropoid, Shapeless, or Bipedal.

The Quadruped body type walks on four legs. These creatures will move in the same way as regular four-legged animals. Four legs give them a great deal of stability, but it usually means that they are shorter in height. To make up for this, they sometimes rear up on their hind legs to attack.

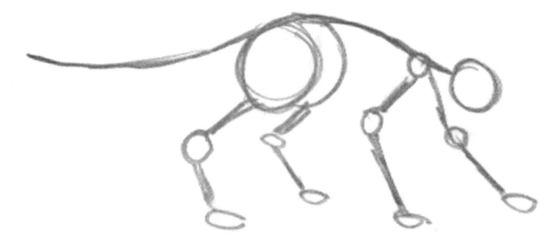

Giant Monsters

Quadruped monsters are particularly suited to stories in which you desire for your monster to convey a bestial character. It is harder to relate to a creature on four legs than on two. There is a wealth of reference to draw from, as the number of four-legged species on Earth is in the thousands.

Another body design is that of the insect-like giant monster, everything from giant ants and spiders to mutant crabs. This body type usually has more than four legs. Since they are creations of your imagination, they can have as many as you want. The fact that we are used to seeing creatures such as this as small and unthreatening adds to their ability to frighten.

Giant Monsters

There are a number of creatures that do not really have a specific category. Sometimes they have no bones, like squid, octopus, or slime. Other monsters have shapes that they alter regularly. A silicon monster made complete sand that doesn't stay in one shape for very long or a Giant Monster made entirely of light would be examples of t Finally, some body shapes, like a snake's, are unique and highly recognizable but not really deserving of their own specification.

Giant Squid are one of the few Giant Monsters that really exist. This can make stories centering on them seem more realistic. Giant sea monsters have a long tradition in most cultures of the world that border on water, so there is a wealth of information to choose from. Anything from sea serpents to man-eating oysters works as a story concept.

Don't feel that a creature's natural environment li its story potential. Nothing shakes up a reader lik unexpected behavior. I highly urge you to take y inspiration, in this case a squid, out of its natural environment and experiment.

In this image, a squid is on land in front of a scho house. This does not agree with what convention knowledge says is true of squid, so one has to wonder in what other ways this squid is unique.

Giant Monsters

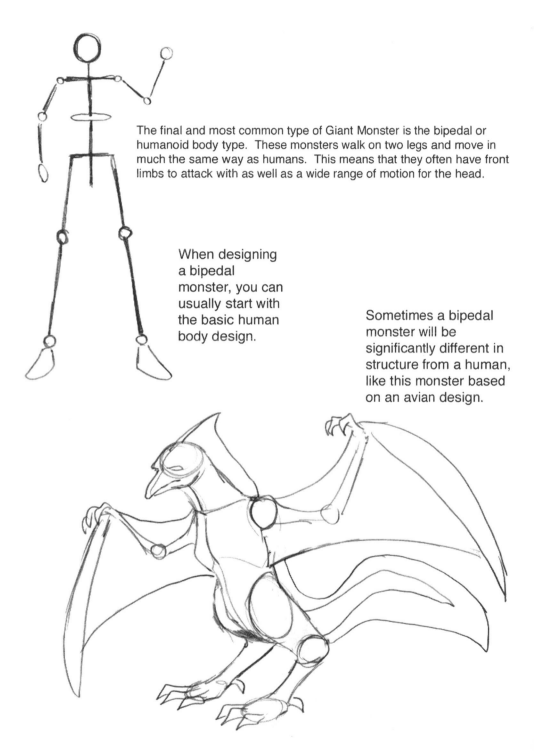

The final and most common type of Giant Monster is the bipedal or humanoid body type. These monsters walk on two legs and move in much the same way as humans. This means that they often have front limbs to attack with as well as a wide range of motion for the head.

When designing a bipedal monster, you can usually start with the basic human body design.

Sometimes a bipedal monster will be significantly different in structure from a human, like this monster based on an avian design.

Giant Monsters

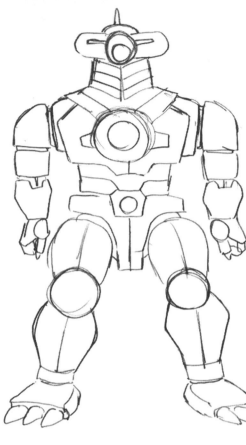

Like all Giant Monsters, bipedal monsters can be anything. Reptilian designs have long been popular, but giant people are not unknown, and neither are robots.

Giant Monsters

Step 1.

When drawing a bipedal Giant Monster, make sure that its shape is balanced. Ask yourself, "Would this creature be able to support its own weight in real life, and would it be able to stand on two legs? Where would its arms be? Would they be attached to its shoulders or somewhere else on its chest?"

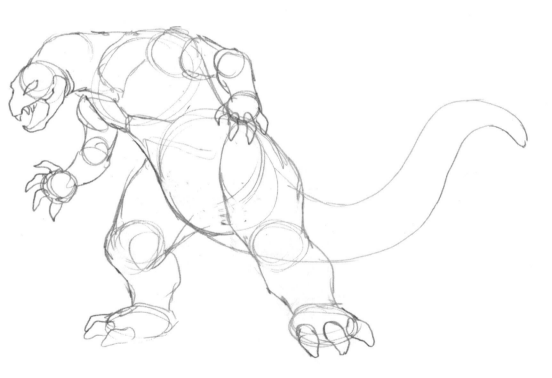

Let's see how a Giant Monster develops step by step. We have decided to draw a very classic design: the Thunder Lizard, a cross between a Tyrannosaurus Rex and a regular lizard. Something about a cold-blooded monster just appeals to me. They are both terrestrial, in that we have encounters with them regularly, and alien, in that they are cold-blooded and totally different from us biologically.

Giant Monsters

Step 2

After establishing the basic shape of our Giant Monster, we can begin to add some details. It is covered with overlapping bone plates for protection, a design element shared with the armadillo. Bony spines along its back, arms, and head give it a mo menacing appearance.

From Step 1 to Step 2, there are a wide range of design choices that can be made. We could have instead chosen to make our Giant Monster sleek and smooth or even hairy. Try photo-copying the previous page and experimenting with different ways of developing the basic shape we laid out.

Giant Monsters

Step 3.

A little rendering develops the different textures of the monster. It is now looking very threatening. There is a clear difference between the plating and the unprotected skin, shown by the addition of the wrinkles in the skin. This image is now ready to be inked.

Variety keeps your monster from looking dull. The different types of plating are the key in this drawing, from the rounded shoulder guard to the breast plate and horned head plate.

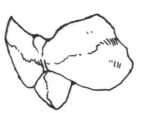

Giant Monsters

Step 4.

After inking your Giant Monster, erase your pencil lines, and you have a gargantuan terror ready to destroy a city, do battle with another mutation of nature, or just scare the local wildlife.

This is just one example, and a fairly traditional one at that, of a Giant Monster. When creating your own, you can draw from the classics or do something totally different. The beauty of monsters is that the newer and more creative, the more interesting and scary they can be.

Giant Monsters

Bipedal monsters can take a great number of shapes. It is very important that you do not become caught up in the idea of making them look human simply because they have two legs. They can have multiple heads, tentacles instead of arms, or wings. It is even okay if they lack certain things that would be expected. A giant bipedal monster without a head would be pretty shocking.

A fight between bipedal monsters is easy to construct and follow visually, since we are used to looking at two upright figures interact.

Giant Monsters

Sniff....Giant Monsters really are beautiful. It just tugs on your heart strings...as you run in terror, of course. Neve forget the running and the terror and the screaming.

But wait...what's this? There's more? What could be better than a Giant Monster in its element? How about all the other variations on this theme? Let's take a look!

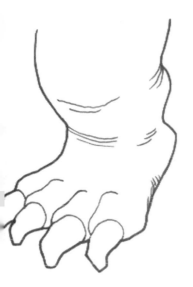

A nice, clawed stomper is great, but there are so many other kinds of feet out there to choose from, some slightly different, others unique to the extreme.

A modified anteater claw! If it's good for dissecting an anthill, why wouldn't it be good for dissecting a building?

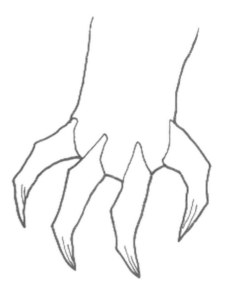

A wing-mounted claw...might not be as effective as a wing-mounted heat-seeking missile, but when you're invincible and 100 feet tall, you're not complaining.

Giant Monsters

I'm gonna get you! Okay, maybe I won't but human hands are pretty good at squashing bugs. Think how much better they would work if they had palms the size of a truck

When you walk on lava, your feet may look a bit different. No one is complaining as long as they remain uncharred.

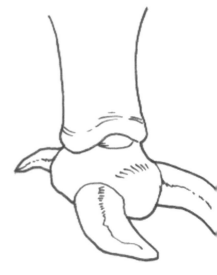

How about a limb that is reverse-jointed? That's something you don't see everyday. Plus, they say the devil is reverse-jointed. Creepy!

Giant Monsters

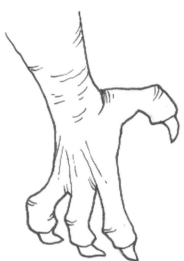

I have never really appreciated my pinkies, so this design appeals to me, although nail-trimming is probably a real problem.

How's this look to you, monkey fans? Great for cradling the damsel of your banana-filled dreams.

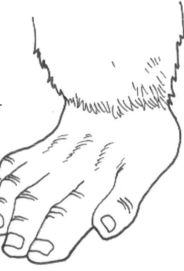

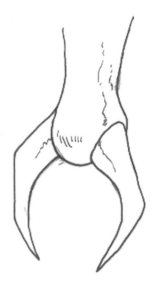

A nice pointy pincer for...pointing and pincing, I guess.

Giant Monsters

Nothing like a trio of rending claws to make a good impression—well, some kind of impression, at least.

A bird's wings look fairly normal, but not when they are attached to a shambling, reptilian bog monster. Although you can stuff a pillow pretty fast with 8-foot feathers.

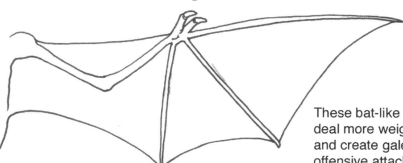

These bat-like wings can carry a grea deal more weight than you would ima and create gale-force winds as an offensive attack.

240

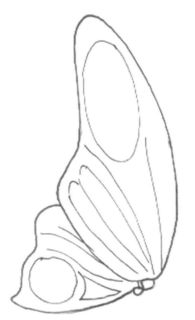

Ahh...the beauty of a butterfly's wing, so colorful, so soft, almost hypnotic. All the better for a Giant Monster who wants to appear unthreatening up until he eats your town hall.

Insect wings beat at a very rapid rate, sometimes moving so fast that they blur into invisibility. They also catch light and filter it into dazzling prismatic displays.

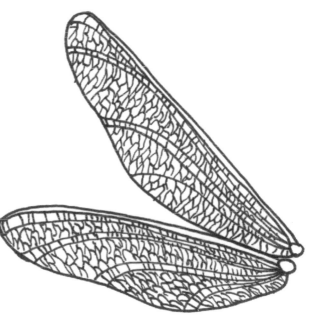

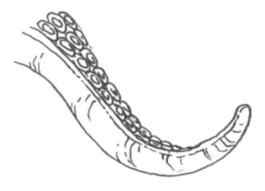

Tentacles! Many is the time I have wished for a few tentacles to help me out during the day. Some creatures have all the luck. They are extremely versatile, and just about any Giant Monster can benefit from a few.

Giant Monsters

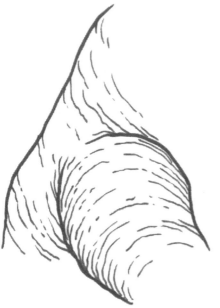

Skin–you got it, I got it, and so do most Giant monsters. Of course, theirs might not be as soft and fragile as ours. They probably have cold-resistant, fireproof, radioactive super skin.

A big concern of the Giant Monster youth of today is skin blemishes, but sometimes the warty look is just something you have to accept.

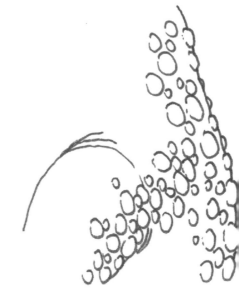

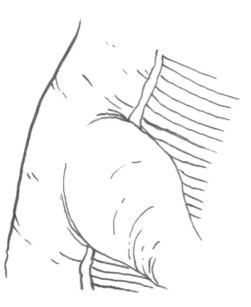

While humans just have one major skin type, Giant Monsters can often have two or three or ten.

Giant Monsters

Scales are great for protection. The way they overlap means that every inch of your body is covered, plus you dry out a lot faster than those Giant Monsters with fur.

Fur is comprised of lots of short hairs that cover most of your body. It can be any color and is very functional. Usually, fur grows at a length suited to a creature's current climate.

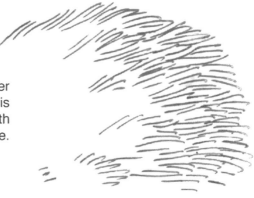

Feathers can be a blessing and a curse. They provide great temperature control, but sometimes you look a little like a sissy. Of course, once you peck someone's head off, that really isn't a concern anymore.

Giant Monsters

When a Giant Monster is hairy, it is covered all over with long hair. his allows a Giant Monster to develop a suitably repunant odor if it stays away from water long enough, and smaller creatures can make their home in its hair. Everybody wins!

Fish scales are great because they are almost always accompanied by a slimy body coating, which comes in real handy when grappling with other Giant Monsters.

Sectional armor can be formed by bone plates, extra-tough leathery skin, oversized scales, or even mineral deposits that have grown on a Giant Monster over the eons. As far as defense goes, this may be th peak, as it provides both maneuverability and protection.

OU CAN DRAW MANGA

Giant Monsters

Sometimes a Giant Monster will wear armor or be built with metal skin or maybe even grow it. A shiny metal exterior requires constant attention in the form of polishing or dips in a boiling natural spring. A good heat-scouring in a lava pit can also do the trick.

Chitin plating is common among insect monsters. It acts both to contain an insect's internal organs and to protect it from aggression. Chitin has been known to have a glossy and shiny appearance which can be quite breathtaking.

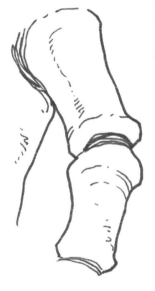

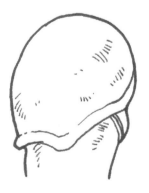

A dull metal exterior can sometimes be the clever deception of a monster trying to appear old and lazy.

Giant Monsters

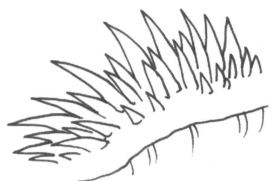

Spiny, porcupine-like skin can be a great defense and when you can shoot your spines at high spee it can also be a great offensive weapon. Nothing says "Stay away" like a four-foot spike of hair.

Aside from spikes, there are a number of other ways that a Giant Monster can be decked out. The classic saurian fin lets others know that you have a respect for tradition, and if it can be used to harness cosmic radiation to be released in a death blast, all the better.

Patches of hairy spines can accent different parts o monster and make grappling uncomfortable f attackers. They can also say, "Hey, look, I have we patches of hairy-looking spines on my body, all fro eating nuclear wast

Giant Monsters

An aquatic fin will help any Giant Monster swim better, and some of them can excrete paralyzing venom, which is a nice perk.

Weathered bone plates can make all kinds of statements, like, "Hey, I spend a lot of time in the ocean and let things grow on me," or "Look, I'm old."

A couple of bone spurs are the bare minimum for any accessorized Giant Monster. You can hang trees and power lines from them, and they are great at saying, "Don't Touch!"

Giant Monsters

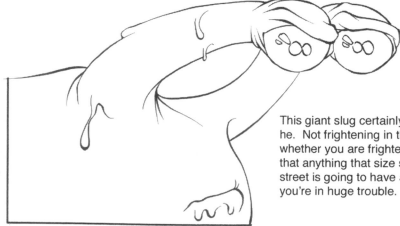

This giant slug certainly doesn't look like much, do he. Not frightening in the least, if you ask me. Sti whether you are frightened or not, you have to adr that anything that size sliming its way down your street is going to have an effect, and if you upset i you're in huge trouble.

Giant Monsters

See! What did I tell you about upsetting a 200-ton slug? Do you have any idea how hard it is to get slug slime out of Main Street?

Giant Monsters

When a giant monster is created by humans, you are pretty much assured that you are in for a rough ride. This monster was the result of a scientist attempting to place his consciousness into a large body of water. It worked. Oh, the joys of modern science. Sadly, the strain of holding himself together has worn this scientist down, and since every time he tries to get close to his machines he shorts them out, he has become pretty agitated. Here's hoping another giant monster with a huge thirst comes along and deals with him, or else this living tidal wave may flood the neighborhood.

One of the nice things about drawing gigantic monsters is that it is okay if the little people have little or no detail. When a monster is truly giant, he will be too big to notice or care about any detail. The key is to get across these three ideas: fleeing, peril, and panic.

giant, shapeless blob can be pretty dangerous, especially when its body is composed of a sh-digesting jelly and it needs to consume hundreds of thousands of calories a day. There isn't really y place you can hide from a monster that is capable of oozing through the smallest cracks or, when at fails, simply digesting its way through any obstacle. Great origins for monsters like this include outer ace, deep beneath the Earth's crust, and your mother's uncleaned garbage disposal.

Notice how even the clothing is digested. This is an economical monster, wasting nothing. Ain't nature neat?

Giant Monsters

This giant monster is dedicated to ruining your beach time. A monster without eyes, a nose, or ears and with a huge mouth is probably only concerned with one thing: eating, and after that, eating some more. The double row of teeth means he is twice as focused on food. This monster would probably fall into the "other" group.

Instead of having sucke its tentacles are covere in the same skin as the rest of its body. This pr ably means that this cre ture can't afford to have any soft skin on its bod

versus

This monster is interesting in that it has tentacles and seems to originate from the ocean.

Giant Monsters

ess of a giant monster and more of a
ant problem, swarm attacks are no
ughing matter. In some respects, the
ive is the giant monster, and when it acts
ith a single mind, it can be more deadly
an any single large creature. A hive of
ller bees can kill a person with rapidity
nd ease. A swarm of locusts will devour
verything and anything in its path. Ants
n a rampage will not only eat everything,
ney will knock down things that are in
neir way. Add a little toxic leakage or
adioactive mutation, and you are dealing
vith a situation that is no small problem.

One bee alone
is a nuisance.
300,000 is
unholy
retribution.

Giant Monsters

Sometimes Giant Monsters seem limited from a storytelling point of view. The immediate conclusion is
rampaging and destroying a city is all they are good for. Nothing could be further from the truth, as the
tinued survival of the genre can attest.

A Giant Monster's motivation is almost always a mystery, because it cannot communicate with humans
The chance exists that a Giant Monster is actually benevolent, but because of its nature it is attacked,
might simply be a foil, its presence being the catalyst for an entirely different story. One of the most vis
exciting ideas is multiple Giant Monsters fighting each other and humans being merely bystanders, see
to understand what they are witnessing.

It is important to try and capture both the terror and sheer magnitude of Giant Monsters as well as their
majesty and awe-inspiring nature.

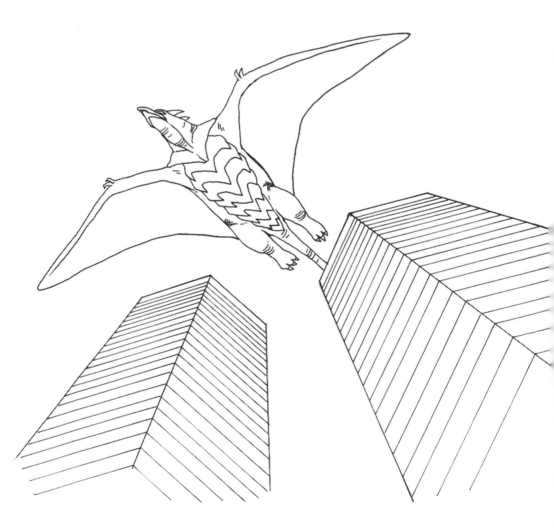

Mecha

ANIMAL LAND MECHA

A wolf is a good form for a quadrupedal (four-legged) land mech.

Mecha

The joints are set up almost as if they were screwed in place. The shoulder and neck joint assemblies are connected, and the neckline is ridged into the shoulder.

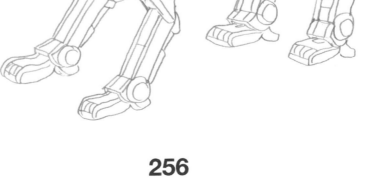

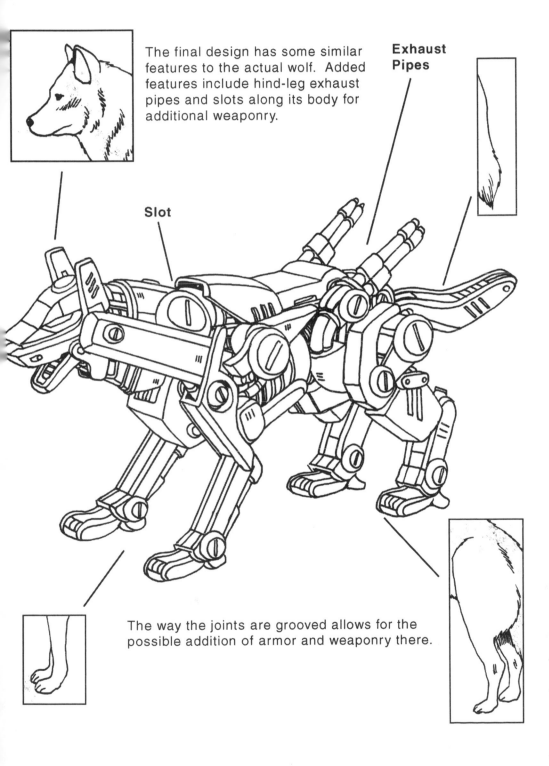

The final design has some similar features to the actual wolf. Added features include hind-leg exhaust pipes and slots along its body for additional weaponry.

Exhaust Pipes

Slot

The way the joints are grooved allows for the possible addition of armor and weaponry there.

Mecha

ANIMAL SEA MECHA

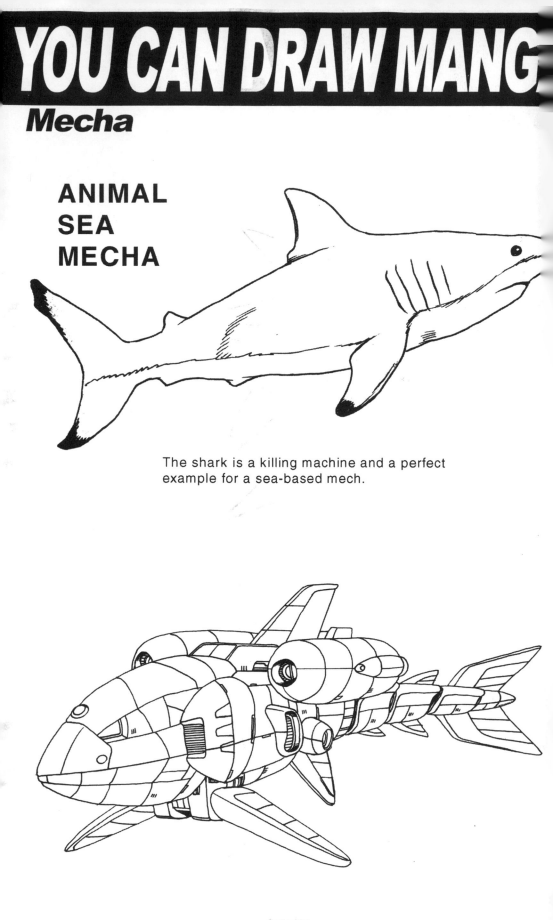

The shark is a killing machine and a perfect example for a sea-based mech.

Mecha

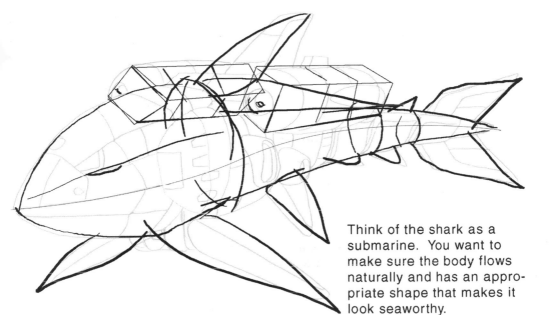

Think of the shark as a submarine. You want to make sure the body flows naturally and has an appropriate shape that makes it look seaworthy.

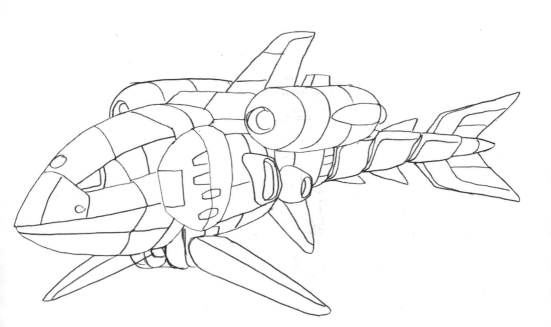

Mecha

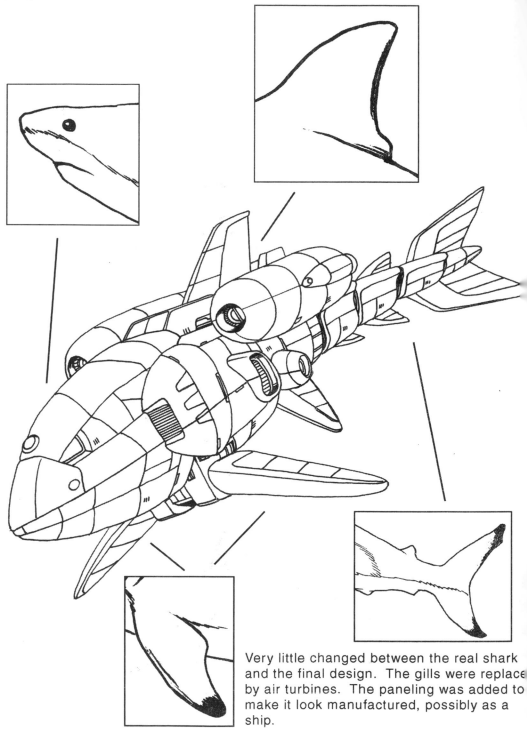

Very little changed between the real shark and the final design. The gills were replaced by air turbines. The paneling was added to make it look manufactured, possibly as a ship.

Mecha

ANIMAL
AIR
MECHA

The hawk is an air-based predator and a good example for air-based mechs.

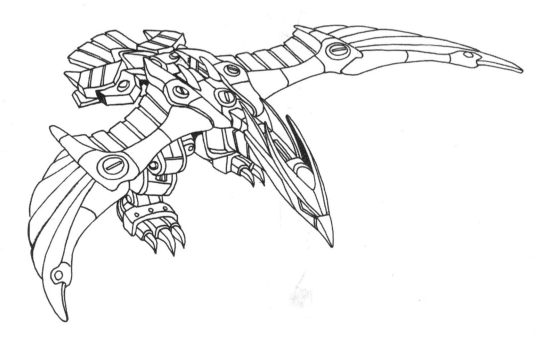

Mecha

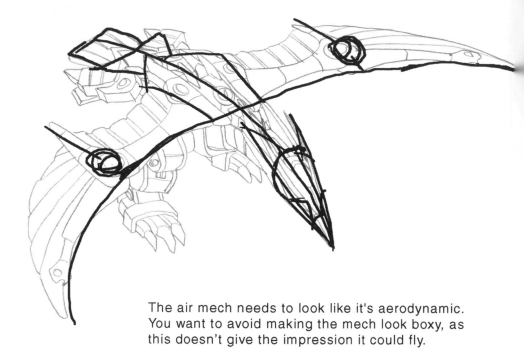

The air mech needs to look like it's aerodynamic. You want to avoid making the mech look boxy, as this doesn't give the impression it could fly.

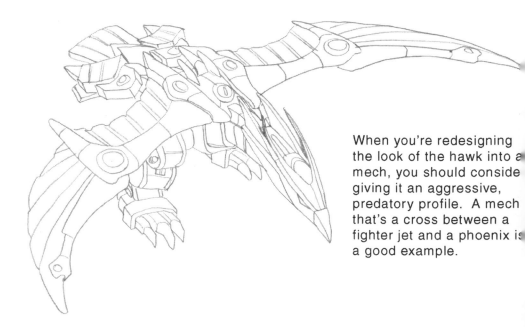

When you're redesigning the look of the hawk into a mech, you should conside giving it an aggressive, predatory profile. A mech that's a cross between a fighter jet and a phoenix is a good example.

Mecha

The tail feathers are simplified to look like a tail fin on a jet.

The streamlined wings give the impression of a fighter jet.

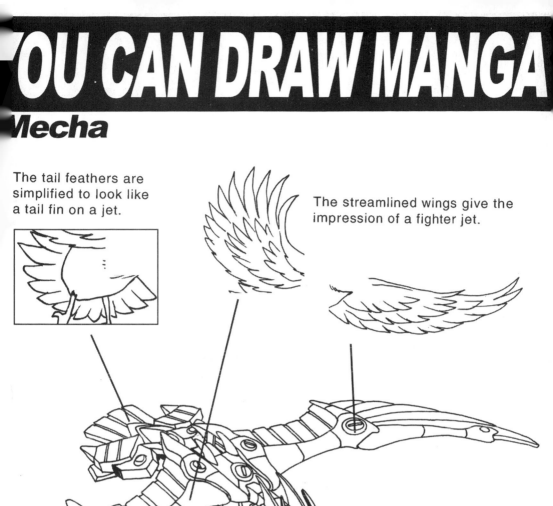

The head represents the cockpit.

The talons, although not aerodynamic, could act as weapons. You could design them to fold into the body while the mech is in flight.

Mecha

ANIMAL GROUND MECHA

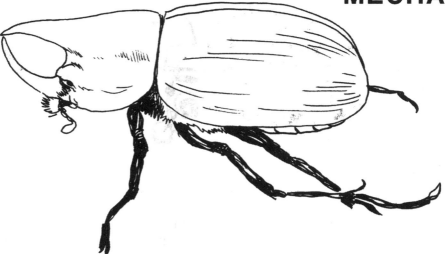

The beetle represents the land mech storm trooper, possibly for off-world combat. It's made to replicate not just the look, but also the behavior of an insect in a particular environment.

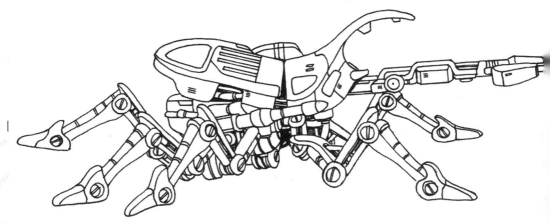

Depending on this mech's size, it could be used for surveillance or (if piloted) ground support.

Mecha

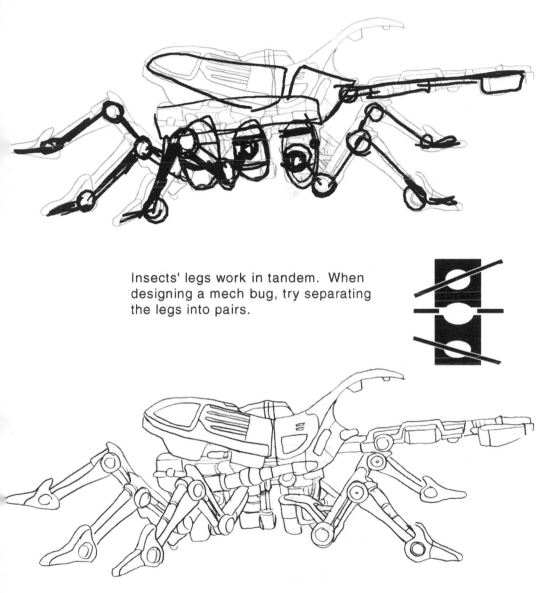

Insects' legs work in tandem. When designing a mech bug, try separating the legs into pairs.

You have six legs here, so the middle pair of legs would be used to keep the center mass stable when the forelegs and hindlegs are in mid-stride.

Mecha

The armor placement would correspond to the beetle's, protecting sensitive equipment -- in this case, the mech's engine.

The abdomen is segmented for movement.

You could make the beetle's horns into a sensor array and gun combination.

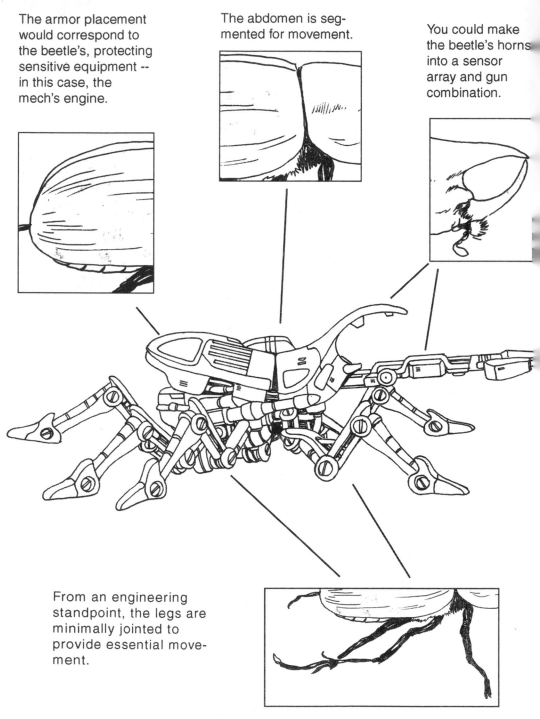

From an engineering standpoint, the legs are minimally jointed to provide essential movement.

266

Magical Effects

Drawing magical effects can look complicated, but by taking a simplified approach and breaking down the effect into its base shapes, you can make any effect simple to illustrate.

Magical Effects

Here we have an example of magic affecting rocks. When drawing this type of effect, try not to worry about the details in the beginning. What you want do is lay out the overall shape of the action as well as the direction the effect is traveling.

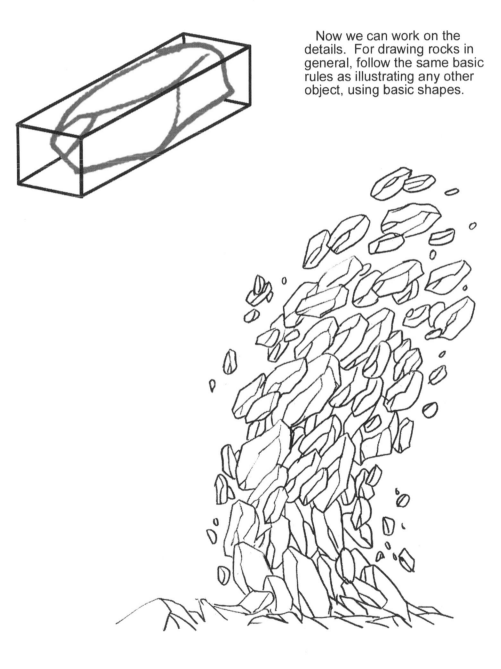

Now we can work on the details. For drawing rocks in general, follow the same basic rules as illustrating any other object, using basic shapes.

Magical Effects

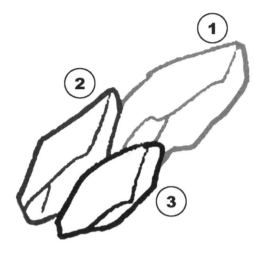

The real trick to drawing the details is overlapping the rocks. Drawing one rock in the front, then a portion of the next rock next to it, followed by another portion of a rock, will give the illusion of depth.

Magical Effects

The second part of creating depth is drawing the rocks towards the bottom, slightly larger than the ones towards the top. This will give the impression that the effect is going up and away from the viewer.

271

Magical Effects

Another fantastic effect is one you don't have to draw. The invisible ball of energy is illustrated by using the background and debris to get the effect across.

Begin by drawing the foreground.

YOU CAN DRAW MANGA

Magical Effects

As you see here, the ball of energy would not only be affecting the debris but the ground as well. So, as you start to render the foreground, place the boulders and other details in a pattern with the diameter of the ball in mind. Keep this in mind for the flying debris as well.

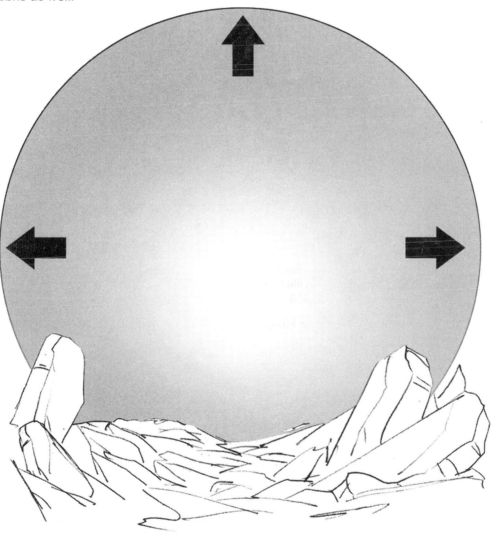

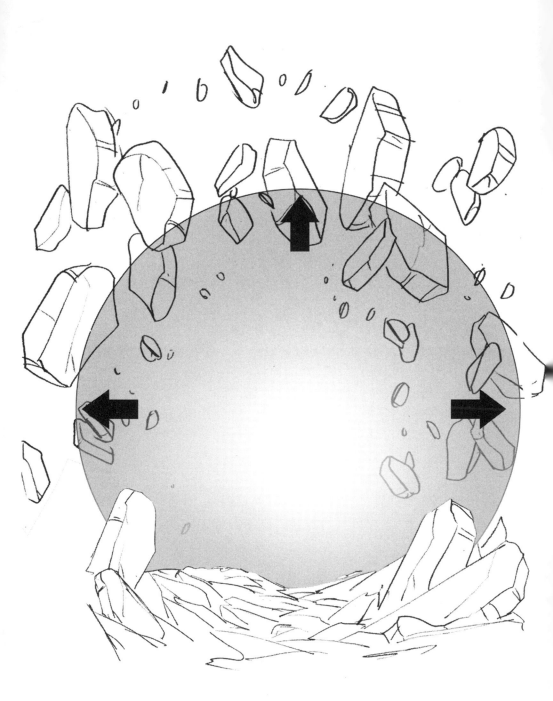

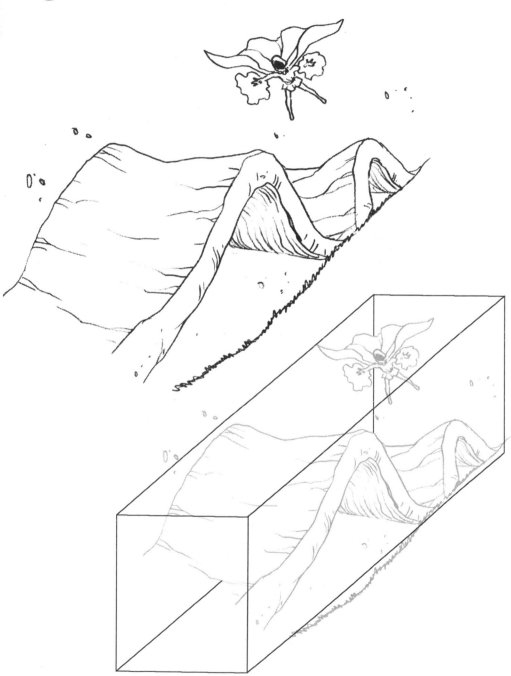

The way to approach illustrating large strips of earth being lifted
is to use the cube to help figure out your perspective first.

Magical Effects

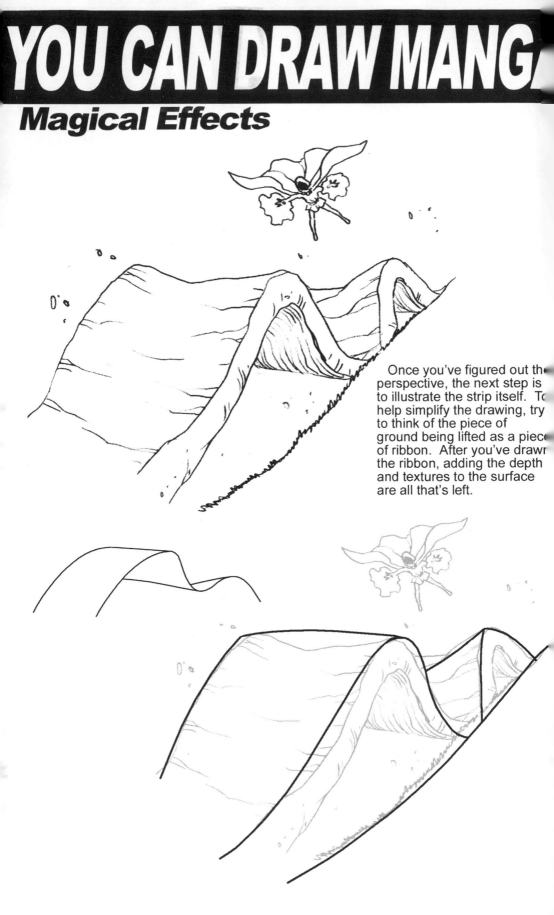

Once you've figured out the perspective, the next step is to illustrate the strip itself. To help simplify the drawing, try to think of the piece of ground being lifted as a piece of ribbon. After you've drawn the ribbon, adding the depth and textures to the surface are all that's left.

Magical Effects

As you can see, many magical effects are rooted in the simplest of basic shapes. It's up to you not to be daunted by trying to come up with new and original effects. On the next few pages is a two-part effect. How were the basic shapes used, and how were they altered to get the desired look?

Magical Effects

In this step of the sequence, the piece of earth is lifted out of the ground. When you are drawing this type of effect, a small detail to note is the shape of the piece. The cone shape is a result of where the magic-user was positioned in relation to the piece that was cut out.

Magical Effects

Finally, as you put them in sequence next to each other, you get an entire effect demonstrating what this person's power can do to a large mass of land.

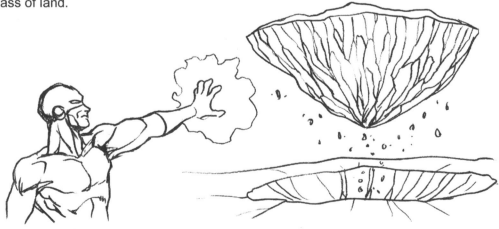

Magical Effects

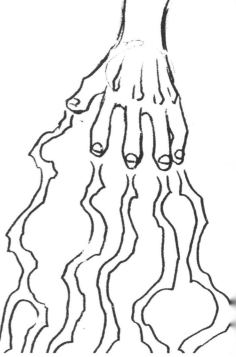

Lightning is one of the simpler effects to illustrate. Basically, it is a line with a series of angles in it. When you are drawing an electric bolt, the real trick is to keep the angles as random-looking as possible. Lightning is a naturally occuring thing, and because it comes from nature, the more random it should look. If the angles you put into your lightning bolt follow a pattern, it will begin to look manufactured. Also, instead of using perfectly straight lines, give them a slight curve, this will help them look more organic.

A helpful tip when illustrating the magical uses of electricity is, when you illustrate the effect, leave a small gap between the bolt and the place where the electricity is coming from. It will help the effect look like it is coming from the object rather than from under it.

280

Magical Effects

When illustrating the use of electricity as a weapon, drawing several bolts coming from the hands will show the viewer that there is alot of energy involved. Compare this to the above effect which uses only a couple of bolts. Which drawing is showing the most power being used?

Magical Effects

Electricity doesn't just have to be used as a weapon, it can also be used as a defense. Balls of energy around the hands or creating energy shields are illustrated simply by drawing the item that is to be created, like a shield, then using what you've learned about illustrating electricity to show where the shield originated.

YOU CAN DRAW MANGA

Perspective

Perspective

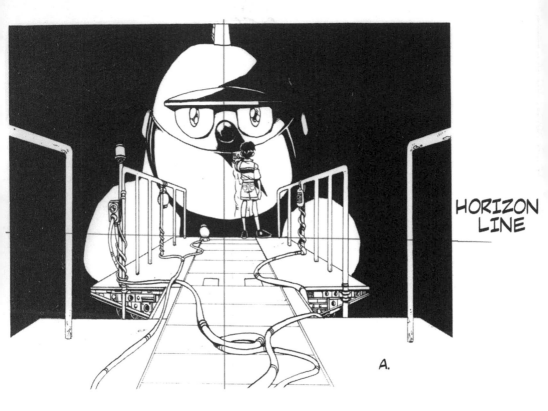

HORIZON
LINE

A.

IMPORTANT NOTE TO REMEMBER: THE HORIZON LINE IS THE VERY FOUNDATION OF PERSPECTIVE. IT CAN BE A VERY POWERFUL TOOL IN DRAWING AND IS THE BASIS FOR ALL REALISTICALLY RENDERED DRAWING. IT WORKS IN FINE ART AS WELL AS IN MANGA, SO IT IS IMPORTANT TO MAKE NOTE OF IT!

EXAMPLE A: HERE I WANTED TO SHOW SCALE BETWEEN THE FOREGROUND OBJECT AND THE BACKGROUND OBJECT.

IN EXAMPLE B,
DISTANCE IS
WHAT I WAS
AIMING FOR.

EXAMPLE C
SHOWS A
CORRELATION
BETWEEN
OBJECTS IN
THE FOREGROUND,
THE MIDDLE
GROUND AND
THE BACKGROUND.

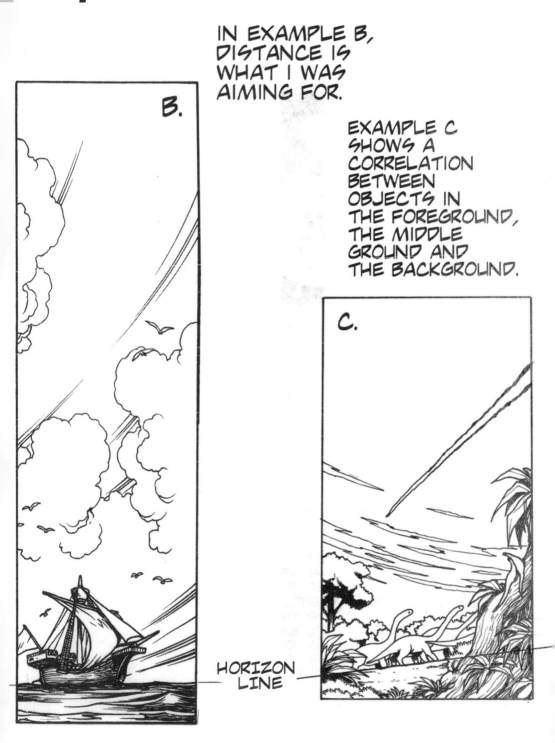

B.

C.

HORIZON
LINE

Perspective

BY USING THE HORIZON LINE
IN EXAMPLE D, YOU CAN ALSO
USE A FORCED PERSPECTIVE.

Perspective

IN DRAWING, PERSPECTIVE IS IMPORTANT IN REALISTIC ART OR DRAMATIC STORYTELLING.

HORIZON LINE

THE HORIZON LINE: THIS IS THE LINE THAT APPEARS AS YOU LOOK OUT INTO THE DISTANT HORIZON. IT SEPARATES LAND FROM SKY.

NORMAL EYE VIEW

THIS HORIZON LINE IS ALWAYS THERE WHEN YOU STAND ON A LEVEL FIEL
THIS LINE CAN BE BLOCKED BY OBJECTS OR DISTORTED BY LIGHT OR HEAT

HORIZON
LINE

AT TIMES THE HORIZON WILL BE ONLY PARTLY VISABLE
AS IN THE ILLUSTRATION. IMAGINE THE HORIZON
LINE STRETCHING BEYOND THE OBSTRUCTIONS.

IN PERSPECTIVE, IT IS IMPORTANT TO ESTABLISH THE VIEWER IN RELATION TO THE HORIZON LINE, AND IT SHOWS THE EYE LEVEL TO THE CHARACTER IN RELATION TO THE DRAWING.

(A)

THE BIRD'S-EYE VIEW

THIS VIEW TAKES THE SUBJECT HIGH ABOVE THE GROUND. PLACING THE HORIZON HIGH ENABLES ONE TO SEE MORE OF THE GROUP. THE HIGHER THE HORIZON LINE, THE HIGHER THE VIEWPOINT. IT GIVES OBJECTS IN THE DISTANCE A SMALLER FEEL.

Perspective

 **THE WORM'S-EYE VIEW**

HORIZON
LINE

THIS PERSPECTIVE IS USED WHEN THE SUBJECT
IS CLOSE TO THE GROUND OR WAY BELOW THE
HORIZON LINE. IT GIVES OBJECTS A LARGER FEEL.

EXAMPLES OF
BIRD'S-EYE VIEW
PERSPECTIVE...

USING THE BIRD'S-EYE
VIEW PERSPECTIVE GIVES
THE SPECTATOR A VISTA
OVER ALL THAT IS IN VIEW.
OFTEN IT IS USED TO
CONVEY VASTNESS,
SCALE AND TERRITORY.

Perspective

IT HELPS PLACE
THE VIEWER IN AN AREA
THAT HE CAN BECOME
FAMILIAR WITH. IT
ALSO GIVES CHARACTERS
A SENSE OF PLACE.

FWOOSH!

Perspective

SIMPLE USE OF PERSPECTIVE
CAN HELP ESTABLISH TIME
AND PLACE. IT CAN GREATLY
INCREASE THE DRAMA OF ANY
GIVEN STORY.

YOU CAN DRAW MANGA
Perspective

REMEMBER THAT ESTABLISHING
THE ENVIRONMENT CAN BRING
A NEW LEVEL TO THE STORY!

YOU CAN DRAW MANGA

Perspective

BEFORE MAKING A PERSPECTIVE DRAWING, YOU MUST IMAGINE WHAT IS CALLED A "PICTURE WINDOW." THIS IS THE IMAGINARY WINDOW BETWEEN THE SPECTATOR AND THE RENDERING.

THIS ASPECT IS FUNDAMENTAL TO ALL OTHER ASPECTS OF PERSPECTIVE DRAWING.

Perspective

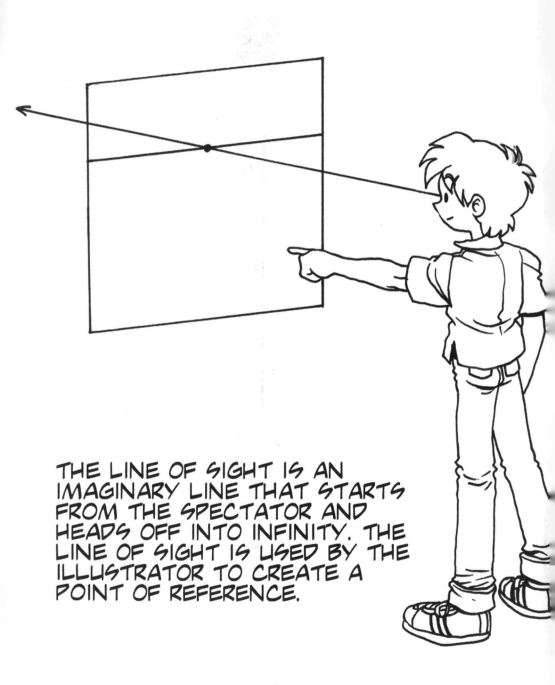

THE LINE OF SIGHT IS AN
IMAGINARY LINE THAT STARTS
FROM THE SPECTATOR AND
HEADS OFF INTO INFINITY. THE
LINE OF SIGHT IS USED BY THE
ILLUSTRATOR TO CREATE A
POINT OF REFERENCE.

Perspective

IN ORDER TO MASTER PERSPECTIVE, IT IS IMPORTANT TO KNOW WHAT IS BEING TALKED ABOUT. BELOW IS A GLOSSARY OF STANDARD PERSPECTIVE TERMS.

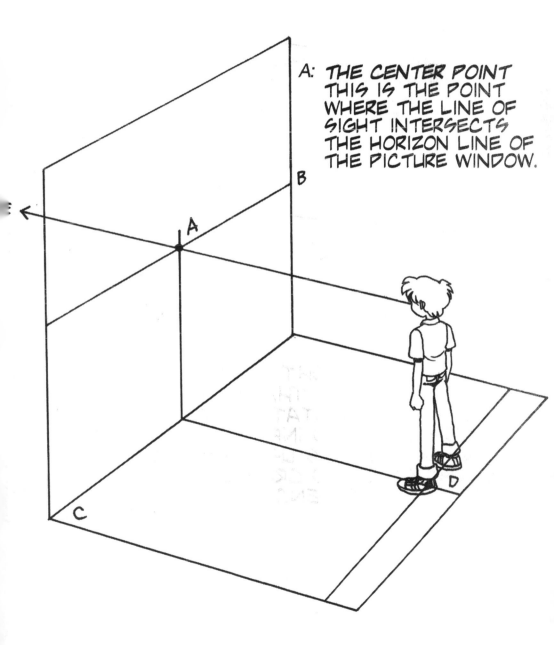

A: THE CENTER POINT THIS IS THE POINT WHERE THE LINE OF SIGHT INTERSECTS THE HORIZON LINE OF THE PICTURE WINDOW.

Perspective

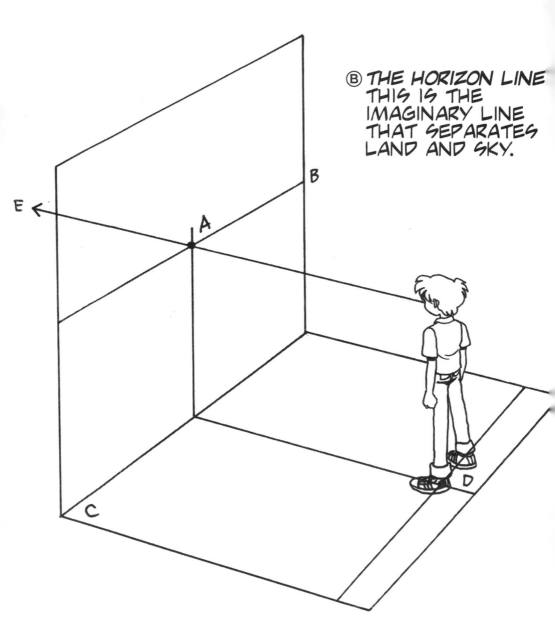

Ⓑ THE HORIZON LINE
THIS IS THE
IMAGINARY LINE
THAT SEPARATES
LAND AND SKY.

Perspective

© *LAND LEVEL*
THIS IS THE HORIZONTAL
LINE THAT SEPARATES
THE PICTURE WINDOW
AND GROUND LEVEL.

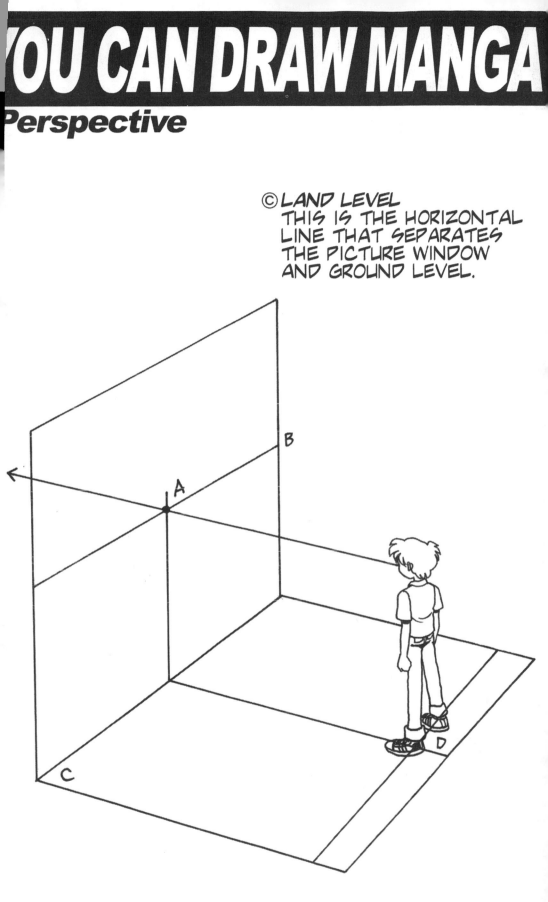

Ⓓ SPECTATOR POINT
THIS IS THE POINT ON THE GROUND LEVEL
WHERE THE SPECTATOR STANDS AND FROM
WHICH THE LINE OF SIGHT STARTS.

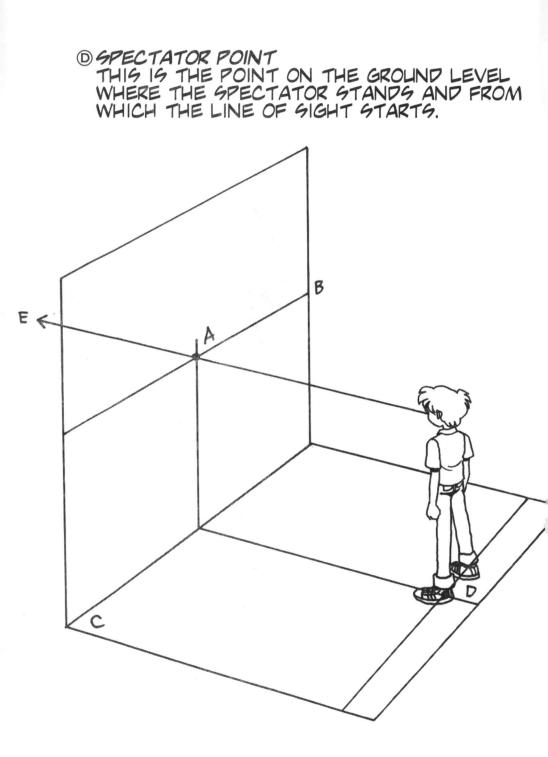

Perspective

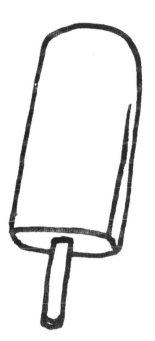

WHEN OBJECTS RECEDE INTO
THE DISTANCE, THEY APPEAR
SMALLER. EQUAL UNITS ALONG
A RECEDING LINE APPEAR TO GET
SMALLER OR "FORESHORTENED." IF
THE AMOUNT OF PERSPECTIVE IS
SLIGHT, THE RATE OF FORESHORT-
ENING IS GRADUAL. IF IT IS GREAT,
THEN THE RATE IS MORE DRAMATIC.

301

YOU CAN DRAW MANGA

Perspective

BY SWITCHING THE VIEWPOINT OF THE SPECTATOR,
AN OBJECT IN VIEW CAN BE CHANGED. THE CLOSER THE
VIEWER GETS TO AN OBJECT, THE MORE FORESHORTENIN.
(SEE SIDE BOX) APPEARS WITHOUT BASICALLY
ALTERING THE SIZE.

SPECTATOR VIEW   SPECTATOR DISTANCE

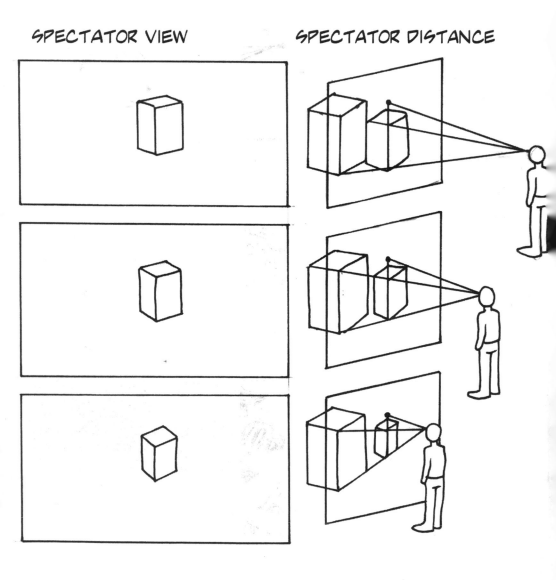

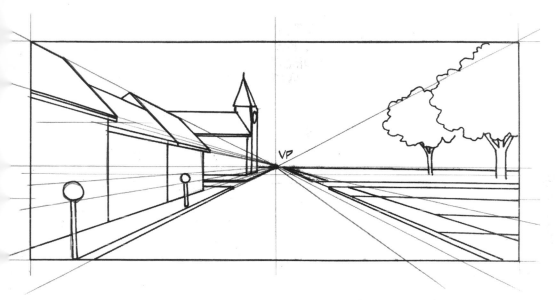

THE POINT ON THE LINE OF SIGHT WHERE ALL PARALLEL LINES RECEDING FROM THE SPECTATOR CONVERGE IS CALLED "THE VANISHING POINT." THIS IS THE POINT FROM WHICH ALL LINES OF PERSPECTIVE START.

YOU CAN DRAW MANGA

Perspective

THE ONE POINT PERSPECTIVE IS THE MOST BASIC FORM
OF DRAWN PERSPECTIVE IN THAT ALL PARALLEL LINES
RETREATING FROM THE SPECTATOR CONVERGE AT
THE VANISHING POINT (VP).

ALL LINES AND PLANES THAT
ARE SQUARE ON, PARALLEL TO,
ON THE PICTURE PLANE (AND THE
OBSERVER) REMAIN PARALLEL AND TO THEIR
TRUE SHAPE WITHOUT DISTORTION OR FORESHORTENING.

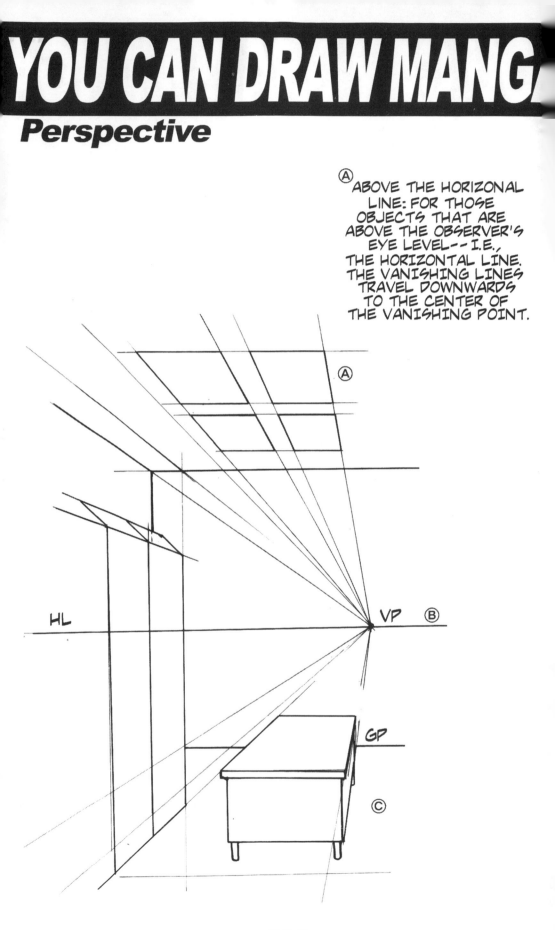

Perspective

Ⓐ ABOVE THE HORIZONAL
LINE: FOR THOSE
OBJECTS THAT ARE
ABOVE THE OBSERVER'S
EYE LEVEL--I.E.,
THE HORIZONTAL LINE.
THE VANISHING LINES
TRAVEL DOWNWARDS
TO THE CENTER OF
THE VANISHING POINT.

Ⓐ

HL

VP   Ⓑ

GP

Ⓒ

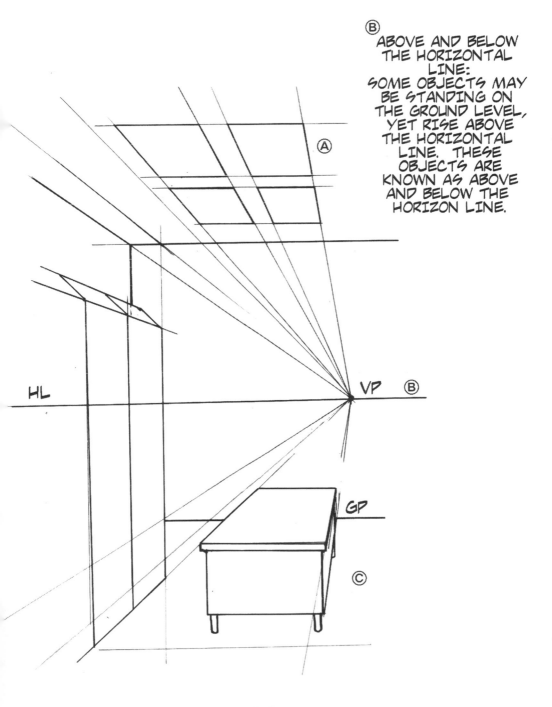

B ABOVE AND BELOW
THE HORIZONTAL
LINE:
SOME OBJECTS MAY
BE STANDING ON
THE GROUND LEVEL,
YET RISE ABOVE
THE HORIZONTAL
LINE. THESE
OBJECTS ARE
KNOWN AS ABOVE
AND BELOW THE
HORIZON LINE.

Perspective

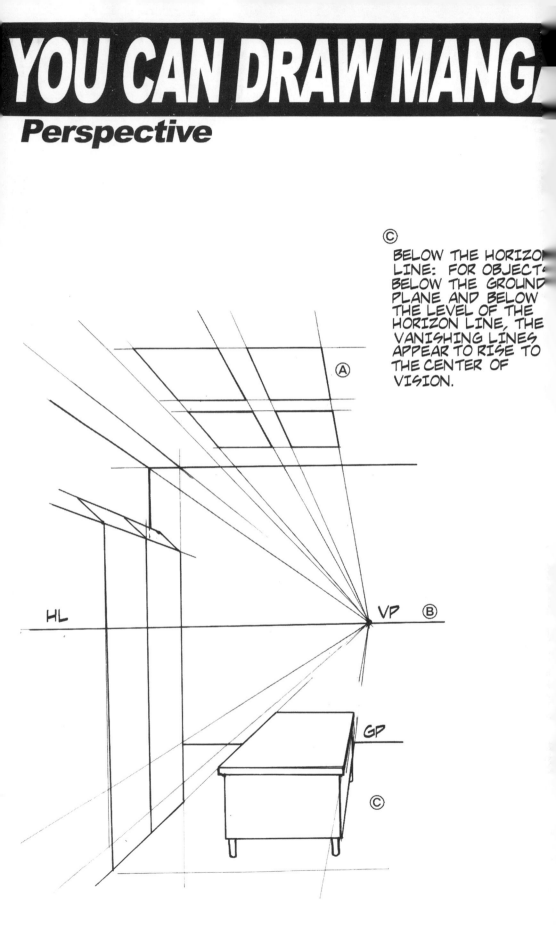

Ⓒ

BELOW THE HORIZON
LINE: FOR OBJECT
BELOW THE GROUND
PLANE AND BELOW
THE LEVEL OF THE
HORIZON LINE, THE
VANISHING LINES
APPEAR TO RISE TO
THE CENTER OF
VISION.

Ⓐ

HL

VP   Ⓑ

GP

Ⓒ

YOU CAN DRAW MANGA

Background

As the old saying goes, "The devil's in the details." When it comes to drawing great backgrounds, it couldn't be more true. In the first image, there are no details in the drawing at all. It's still a good drawing, but there is no texture or anything to separate the different planes of the drawing.

Here's the same drawing, all dressed up! Take the time to observe the textures in nature. They add an extra dimension of depth and richness to your drawing. Be sure your background details don't interfere with your foreground. Use a finer pen when drawing them.

Background

Anyone can draw a building. What makes it a mansion is the little things. Let's draw!

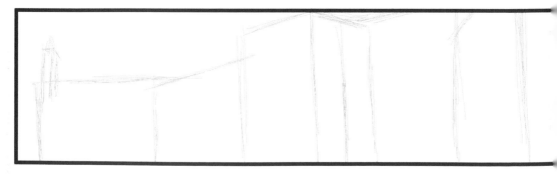

First you want to start with the basic shapes. Remember that all your perspective rules apply. Make sure that when you're laying out the shapes, you use a light line so they'll be easier to erase later.

Background

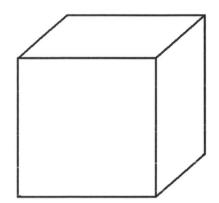

As you can see here, always treat the basic shapes of any building as three-dimensional shapes.

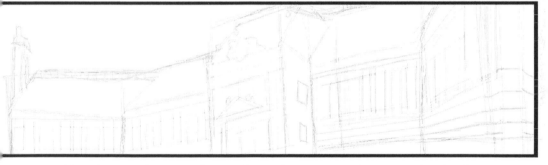

Now that you have the layout done, the next step is to start drawing in the structure of the exteriors. Be sure to indicate the ornaments, windows and other details.

This is the time when you might want to break out the ruler. Using the sketched-in lines of your layout, follow them with the ruler to clean them up, as well as to make them look more "manufactured" like an actual house would be. Then clean up the sketch lines with an eraser so all you have left is the nice, straight lines done with your ruler.

Background

Inking time! This step is important because this is your last chance to fix any perspective or other problems you might have noticed in the drawing phase.

And *voila`*-you're done!

Background

Detailed backgrounds are difficult to draw but are very rewarding. Different cultures have different things about their environments that make them distinctive from other cultures. Here, notice the corners of the roof of this building. Using reference from the area helped make the drawing look more like Japan rather than just another house. The same can be said for the illustration on the bottom of the page.

Background

Things that you wold normally take for granted as a viewer are a must for the artist. Details like the stone steps, the soffits (the visible underside of the roof), or the trees in the foreground all are important pieces, and though they are taken for granted if done well, they would be noticed if they were drawn poorly or not at all.

Background

Ah, now for something a little more familiar. This scene is brought to you by Any Town, U.S.A., and is one of the easier settings to draw. The reason it's easier is because you probably live in a house like this or at least something similar.

These are the two main texture themes in this illustration. You probably didn't notice them at first, but you would have missed them if they weren't there.

Something to remember is that if the locale you're drawing is a regular setting for your story, you should learn to draw it from different angles.

How do ya like the front porch?

Background

The inside of the house you create should be just as detailed, if not more so, than the outside. Again, draw from what you know and really pay attention to the little things, because, after all, it's those things that'll sell it. Notice how the sofa has things on it like a throw blanket and an arm rest cover. Things like stuffed animals tell you about a character even before you meet them.

Background

Here's more of the house. As mentioned before, if this is a recurring backdrop for your stories, you may want to plan out the house and figure out what the rooms look like on the inside.

The difference between homey settings and massive interiors is scale. If you notice, the room could actually be any size. The thing that gives any sense of scale is the people inside the dance hall.

Another trick to making ordinary interiors appear to be an elegant mansion from the inside is giant windows. For some reason, big windows say "expensive house." Don't fight it, just be thankful for the assumption!

Of course, the most obvious way to get across "expensive" is to draw the furniture. Large fireplaces, pianos and Chippendale chairs automatically say "upper crust."

319

Background

From the upper crust to the bottom of the barrel! Something else that is important to know how to illustrate is how to make something dirty. Being able to age something is helpful when trying to create a certain mood or emphasize a dark, secret location. Cracks, stains, and flaking paint can all be depicted by a few well-placed lines.

Textures and shading are a big part of the basement/underground hideout setting.

Boxes and other clutter can also help in getting the point across.

Background

However you look at it, though, settings and backgrounds are just as important as any character in your cast, so you should take the time to learn how to draw backgrounds as well as props. Once you've mastered referencing backgrounds from reality...

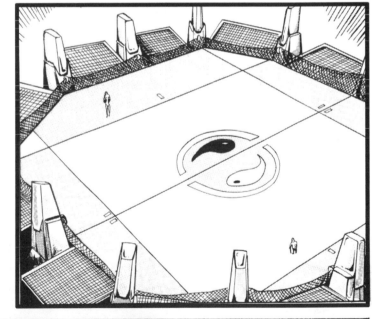

Background

…you can move on to creating the unimagined and strange new worlds of your mind.

The first item on the list of important things to create sweeping fantasy backgrounds is trees.

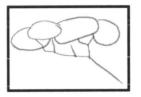

When you draw trees, it is always easiest to use simple lines to figure out the branches first. Then, using ovals, you can lay out the bulk of the leaves. When you draw out the leaves, treating them as a whole mass will be simpler and take less time than drawing individual leaves on your tree.

Fantasy Background

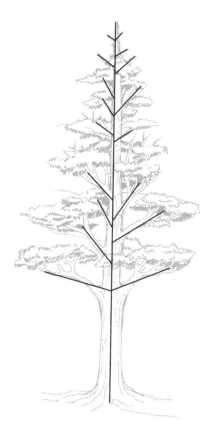

We begin by drawing a vertical line to represent the trunk, then we draw smaller diagonal lines for the branches. Notice that the lines for the branches aren't perfectly horizontal. That's because the branches of a tree typically grow towards the sky. The branches are also asymmetrical. Drawing them that way will give your tree a more organic look.

After you've laid out the structure of the tree, it's time for the bulk. Begin by fleshing out the trunk and branches. This would be a great time to take a look at your reference to see how the overall shape of a tree looks. Then you can work out where the masses of leaves will be by using ovals.

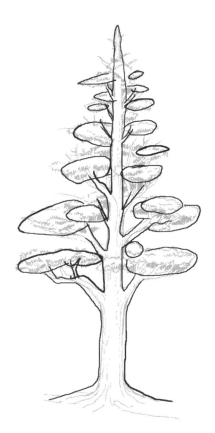

Fantasy Background

Now you can replace the lines of the ovals with "leaf-like" lines and add your blacks to show that the masses of the leaves have depth. Detail lines in the trunk add texture and fill in empty space on the tree.

Fantasy Background

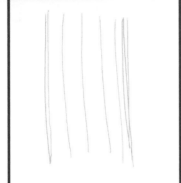

Detailing a tree trunk is sometimes simply erasing the right lines. Here, we begin with drawing a rectangle for the tree trunk. We add unevenly spaced vertical lines on the trunk. Keep in mind that the less perfect you make these lines, the more "real" and "natural" your trees will look.

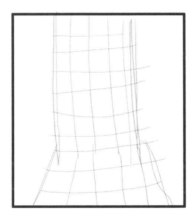

Next, draw unevenly spaced horizontal lines. You have created a rough grid for the bark of your tree.

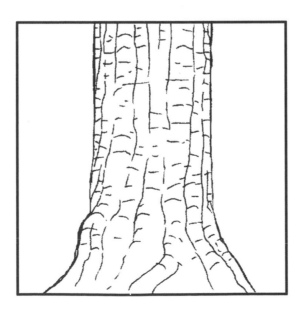

Now, when you get to the inking phase, draw the vertical lines using a slightly wavy and broken line. The horizontal lines should be broken as well and not touch any two successive vertical lines. Also, it's a good idea not to draw every horizontal line: space them out, group a couple close together...
the key is to make it look as random as possible.

Fantasy Background

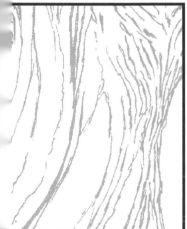

Another approach to drawing tree bark is to repeat the contours of the outside shape of the tree.

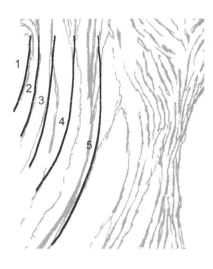

By taking the trunk line on the left and repeating it, working towards the center, then starting again with the right trunk line and repeating **that** line, working towards the center, you will produce a twisting tree bark look.

When it comes time to ink, the broken line technique will complete the organic look of the bark.

Fantasy Background

Moss and vines are other elements that you can add to the trunk of your tree to add more life and detail. As in the last example, begin with the shape of the trunk.

Then you can start sketching in lines to represent where your vines are going to be growing. Then, use "leafy" lines to sketch in the moss and other plant-life that is growing on your tree.

Adding this type of detail speaks to the viewer by saying that this tree is very old and has probably been here for a century or two.

328

Fantasy Background

Mountains are another element you may come across while creating your fantasy world. Mountains, believe it or not, are very easy to draw. Of course, perfecting them is what takes time and effort.

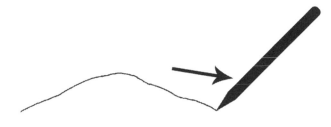

After figuring out where your horizon line is, begin by drawing a really wide-based triangle. When you draw this triangle, don't give it the traditional "pointy" top, give it more of a rounded or even a slightly flattened top. Also, don't worry about making the lines perfectly straight--the rougher, the better.

As you can see from the example lines here, you will be better served by using a rough "shaky" line for the sides of your mountain.

Fantasy Background

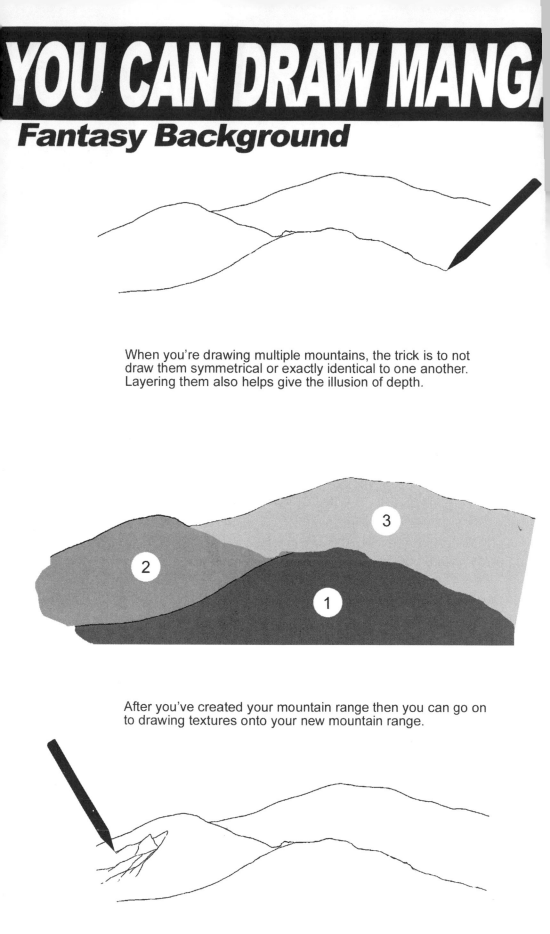

When you're drawing multiple mountains, the trick is to not draw them symmetrical or exactly identical to one another. Layering them also helps give the illusion of depth.

After you've created your mountain range then you can go on to drawing textures onto your new mountain range.

Fantasy Background

Now we can start to add the texture to the mountain. First, we're going to take our mountain shape and remove chunks out of the sides to give the mountain a little depth.

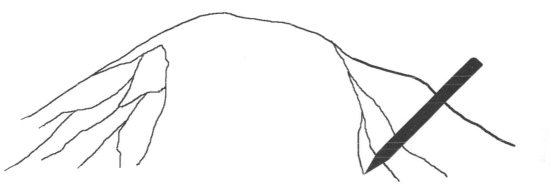

From your inital lines, draw smaller lines that branch off. Basically, you're drawing cracks in the mountain, so keep your lines random. Then, just repeat for all the other mountains in your illustration. Remember, try to keep it as random-looking as possible.

Fantasy Background

Now that you can illustrate the different elements, you can add them together to create a fantastic landscape worthy of any fantasy character you create!

Fantasy Background

As you can see from this example, all the elements are the same, they're just re-arranged.

You want to start with the farthest elements first. In this case, we'll draw the mountains slightly off to the left.

Then we lay in the tree line using simple vertical lines to represent the trunks of the trees. We're keeping the triangle theme when drawing in our tree line. By having the tree line start high right and go down and to the left and the mountains high left and go down to the bottom right, this helps center the viewer's focus towards the middle of the panel.

Fantasy Background

Here's how to draw another type of forest. Bamboo is really common in many manga stories. The image above looks very complex, but actually it isn't. You just have to approach it one line at a time- literally! Start with a single vertical line, followed by a second line parallel to the first. The distance between the two depends on how thick you want to make your piece of bamboo. When you're illustrating a whole forest, you want to make the bamboo different widths. Then, draw the segments that bamboo has. Most times, the bamboo segments are almost the same size. When you draw the lines for the segments, you want to draw them slightly curved to show that the bamboo stalk is actually round.

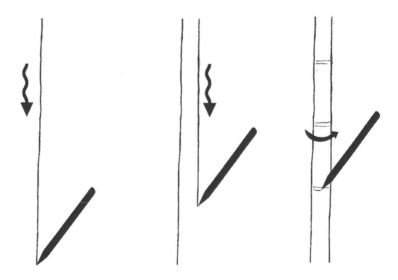

Fantasy Background

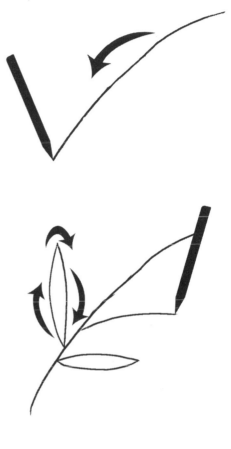

When drawing bamboo leaves, you follow the same general principles as when you illustrate trees, just on a smaller scale. The stalks for the leaves grow from the "knuckles" between the bamboo segments. Begin with a thin, curved line for the stalk. Then, one at a time, draw the leaves using an oval shape that's slightly pointed at the end farthest from the stalk. The outer tips of the leaves will be pointing up and away from the base of the stalk, and the placement of the leaves is asymmetrical.

335

Fantasy Background

As we mentioned before, this background may look complex, but after breaking down exactly how to draw an individual bamboo plant, it's only as complex as how tall you want the plants and how dense you want your bamboo forest to be.

Fantasy Background

What would background be without foreground? In many cases, foreground is an important part of your scene. In fantasy stories, the foreground could be a hut, a castle, boulders, or as in this case, a sign. Oftentimes, signs are made from wood or stone in fantasy stories, so we'll make this one out of wood.

Start by drawing the basic geometric shape of your sign.

After you've drawn the geometric shape, you can begin cutting away to the actual shape you want your sign to be.

Fantasy Background

Now that you have the shape of the sign drawn, you can begin adding details. To show that this is an ancient sign, you may want to use the vine and moss technique on the sign posts. For the main part of the sign there is a lot of room for texturing. Since this sign is made of wood, drawing a wood texture in the empty space will help illustrate that better. Begin by deciding which way the wood grain will go. For signs this long, it usually goes horizontally. Then, draw a series of thin lines horizontally across the sign. Imperfect, broken lines are best for this effect.

Fantasy Background

All you have left is to draw in your background. Usually, when
you're actually drawing a setting like this you will want to draw
the background first, or, if it makes you more comfortable,
draw it on a separate piece of paper, then trace it onto your
final page.

YOU CAN!
DRAW
MECHA
PICK
JP YOUR
COPY TODAY
ww.antarctic-press.com

Gold Digger Pocketmangas
ANTARCTIC PRESS
POCKET MANGA
GOLD DIGGER
FRED PERRY
1
3
4
Catch yours today!
www.antarctic-press.com